In Morocco

IN MOROCCO

From a photograph from the Service des Beaux-Arts au Maroc

Fez Elbali from the ramparts

IN MOROCCO

BY
EDITH WHARTON

ILLUSTRATED

NEW YORK
CHARLES SCRIBNER'S SONS
1920

THE SCRIBNER PRESS

TO

GENERAL LYAUTEY

RESIDENT GENERAL OF FRANCE IN MOROCCO AND TO
MADAME LYAUTEY,

THANKS TO WHOSE KINDNESS THE JOURNEY
I HAD SO LONG DREAMED OF
SURPASSED WHAT I HAD DREAMED

PREFACE

I

HAVING begun my book with the statement that Morocco still lacks a guide-book, I should have wished to take a first step toward remedying that deficiency.

But the conditions in which I travelled, though full of unexpected and picturesque opportunities, were not suited to leisurely study of the places visited. The time was limited by the approach of the rainy season, which puts an end to motoring over the treacherous trails of the Spanish zone. In 1918, owing to the watchfulness of German submarines in the Straits and along the northwest coast of Africa, the trip by sea from Marseilles to Casablanca, ordinarily so easy, was not to be made without much discomfort and loss of time. Once on board the steamer, passengers were often kept in port (without leave to land) for six or eight days; therefore for any one bound by a time-limit, as most war-workers were, it was necessary to travel across country, and to be back at Tangier before the November rains.

This left me only one month in which to visit Morocco from the Mediterranean to the High Atlas, and from the Atlantic to Fez, and even had there been a Djinn's carpet to carry me, the multiplicity of impressions received would have made precise observation difficult.

The next best thing to a Djinn's carpet, a military motor, was at my disposal every morning; but war conditions imposed restrictions, and the wish to use the minimum of petrol often stood in the way of the second visit which alone makes it possible to carry away a definite and detailed impression.

These drawbacks were more than offset by the advantage of making my quick trip at a moment unique in the history of the country; the brief moment of transition between its virtually complete subjection to European authority, and the fast approaching hour when it is thrown open to all the banalities and promiscuities of modern travel.

Morocco is too curious, too beautiful, too rich

in landscape and architecture, and above all too
much of a novelty, not to attract one of the main
streams of spring travel as soon as Mediterranean
passenger traffic is resumed. Now that the war is
over, only a few months' work on roads and railways divide it from the great torrent of "tourism";
and once that deluge is let loose, no eye will ever
again see Moulay Idriss and Fez and Marrakech as
I saw them.

In spite of the incessant efforts of the present
French administration to preserve the old monuments of Morocco from injury, and her native arts
and industries from the corruption of European
bad taste, the impression of mystery and remoteness which the country now produces must inevitably vanish with the approach of the "Circular
Ticket." Within a few years far more will be
known of the past of Morocco, but that past will
be far less visible to the traveller than it is to-day.
Excavations will reveal fresh traces of Roman and
Phenician occupation; the remote affinities between Copts and Berbers, between Bagdad and
Fez, between Byzantine art and the architecture
of the Souss, will be explored and elucidated; but,

PREFACE

while these successive discoveries are being made,
the strange survival of mediæval life, of a life contemporary with the crusaders, with Saladin, even
with the great days of the Caliphate of Bagdad,
which now greets the astonished traveller, will
gradually disappear, till at last even the mysterious autocthones of the Atlas will have folded
their tents and silently stolen away.

II

Authoritative utterances on Morocco are not
wanting for those who can read them in French;
but they are to be found mainly in large and often
inaccessible books, like M. Doutté's "En Tribu,"
the Marquis de Segonzac's remarkable explorations
in the Atlas, or Foucauld's classic (but unobtain-
able) "Reconnaissance au Maroc"; and few, if
any, have been translated into English.

M. Louis Châtelain has dealt with the Roman
ruins of Volubilis and M. Tranchant de Lunel, M.
Raymond Koechlin, M. Gaillard, M. Ricard, and
many other French scholars, have written of Moslem architecture and art in articles published either
in "France-Maroc," as introductions to catalogues

of exhibitions, or in the reviews and daily papers. Pierre Loti and M. André Chevrillon have reflected, with the intensest visual sensibility, the romantic and ruinous Morocco of yesterday; and in the volumes of the "Conférences Marocaines," published by the French government, the experts gathered about the Resident-General have examined the industrial and agricultural Morocco of tomorrow. Lastly, one striking book sums up, with the clearness and consecutiveness of which French scholarship alone possesses the art, the chief things to be said on all these subjects, save that of art and archæology. This is M. Augustin Bernard's volume, "Le Maroc," the one portable and compact yet full and informing book since Leo Africanus described the bazaars of Fez. But M. Augustin Bernard deals only with the ethnology, the social, religious and political history, and the physical properties, of the country; and this, though "a large order," leaves out the visual and picturesque side, except in so far as the book touches on the always picturesque life of the people.

For the use, therefore, of the happy wanderers who may be planning a Moroccan journey, I have added to the record of my personal impressions a slight sketch of the history and art of the country. In extenuation of the attempt I must add that the chief merit of this sketch will be its absence of originality. Its facts will be chiefly drawn from the pages of M. Augustin Bernard, M. H. Saladin, and M. Gaston Migeon, and the rich sources of the "Conférences Marocaines" and the articles of "France-Maroc." It will also be deeply indebted to information given on the spot by the brilliant specialists of the French administration, to the Marquis de Segonzac, with whom I had the good luck to travel from Rabat to Marrakech and back; to M. Alfred de Tarde, editor of "France-Maroc"; to M. Tranchant de Lunel, director of the French School of Fine Arts in Morocco; to M. Goulven, the historian of Portuguese Mazagan; to M. Louis Châtelain, and to the many other cultivated and cordial French officials, military and civilian, who, at each stage of my journey, did their amiable best to answer my questions and open my eyes.

NOTE

In the writing of proper names and of other Arab words the French spelling has been followed.

In the case of proper names, and names of cities and districts, this seems justified by the fact that they occur in a French colony, where French usage naturally prevails; and to spell *Oudjda* in the French way, and *koubba*, for instance, in the English form of *kubba*, would cause needless confusion as to their respective pronunciation. It seems therefore simpler, in a book written for the ordinary traveller, to conform altogether to French usage.

TABLE OF CONTENTS

ILLUSTRATIONS

ILLUSTRATIONS

MAP

I

RABAT AND SALÉ

I

RABAT AND SALÉ

I

LEAVING TANGIER

TO step on board a steamer in a Spanish port, and three hours later to land in *a country without a guide-book*, is a sensation to rouse the hunger of the repletest sight-seer.

The sensation is attainable by any one who will take the trouble to row out into the harbour of Algeciras and scramble onto a little black boat headed across the straits. Hardly has the rock of Gibraltar turned to cloud when one's foot is on the soil of an almost unknown Africa. Tangier, indeed, is in the guide-books; but, cuckoo-like, it has had to lays its egg in strange nests, and the traveller who wants to find out about it must acquire a work dealing with some other country—Spain or Portugal or Algeria. There is no guide-book to Morocco, and no way of knowing, once one has left Tangier behind, where the long trail over the

Rif is going to land one, in the sense understood by any one accustomed to European certainties. The air of the unforeseen blows on one from the roadless passes of the Atlas.

This feeling of adventure is heightened by the contrast between Tangier—cosmopolitan, frowsy, familiar Tangier, that every tourist has visited for the last forty years—and the vast unknown just beyond. One has met, of course, travellers who have been to Fez; but they have gone there on special missions, under escort, mysteriously, perhaps perilously; the expedition has seemed, till lately, a considerable affair. And when one opens the records of Moroccan travellers written within the last twenty years, how many, even of the most adventurous, are found to have gone beyond Fez? And what, to this day, do the names of Meknez and Marrakech, of Mogador, Saffi or Rabat, signify to any but a few students of political history, a few explorers and naturalists? Not till within the last year has Morocco been open to travel from Tangier to the Great Atlas, and from Moulay Idriss to the Atlantic. Three years ago Christians were being massacred in the streets of Salé, the pirate town across the river from Rabat, and two years ago no European had been allowed to enter the Sacred City of Moulay Idriss, the burial-place of the lawful descendant of Ali, founder of the Idrissite dynasty. Now, thanks to the energy and the imagination of one of the greatest of colonial administrators, the country, at least in the French zone, is as safe and open as the opposite shore of Spain. All that remains is to tell the traveller how to find his way about it.

Ten years ago there was not a wheeled vehicle in Morocco; now its thousands of miles of trail, and its hundreds of miles of firm French roads, are travelled by countless carts, omnibuses and motor-vehicles. There are light railways from Rabat to Fez in the west, and to a point about eighty-five kilometres from Marrakech in the south; and it is possible to say that within a year a regular railway system will connect eastern Morocco with western Algeria, and the ports of Tangier and Casablanca with the principal points of the interior.

What, then, prevents the tourist from instantly taking ship at Bordeaux or Algeciras and letting loose his motor on this new world? Only the temporary obstacles which the war has everywhere put in the way of travel. Till these are lifted it will hardly be possible to travel in Morocco except by favour of the Resident-General; but, normal conditions once restored, the country will be as accessible, from the straits of Gibraltar to the Great Atlas, as Algeria or Tunisia.

To see Morocco during the war was therefore to see it in the last phase of its curiously abrupt transition from remoteness and danger to security and accessibility; at a moment when its aspect and its customs were still almost unaffected by European influences, and when the "Christian" might taste the transient joy of wandering unmolested in cities of ancient mystery and hostility, whose inhabitants seemed hardly aware of his intrusion.

II

THE TRAIL TO EL-KSAR

WITH such opportunities ahead it was impossible, that brilliant morning of September, 1917, not to be off quickly from Tangier, impossible to do justice to the pale-blue town piled up within brown walls against the thickly-foliaged gardens of "the Mountain," to the animation of its market-place and the secret beauties of its steep Arab streets. For Tangier swarms with people in European clothes, there are English, French and Spanish signs above its shops, and cab-stands in its squares; it belongs, as much as Algiers, to the familiar dog-eared world of travel—and there, beyond the last dip of "the Mountain," lies the world of mystery, with the rosy dawn just breaking over it. The motor is at the door and we are off.

The so-called Spanish zone, which encloses internationalized Tangier in a wide circuit of territory, extends southward for a distance of about a hundred and fifteen kilometres. Consequently, when good roads traverse it, French Morocco will be reached in less than two hours by motor-travellers bound for the south. But for the present Spanish enterprise dies out after a few miles of macadam (as it does even between Madrid and Toledo), and the tourist is committed to the *piste*. These *pistes* —the old caravan-trails from the south—are more available to motors in Morocco than in southern Algeria and Tunisia, since they run mostly over soil which, though sandy in part, is bound together by a tough dwarf vegetation, and not over pure desert sand. This, however, is the utmost that can be said of the Spanish *pistes*. In the French protectorate constant efforts are made to keep the trails fit for wheeled traffic, but Spain shows no sense of a corresponding obligation.

After leaving the macadamized road which runs south from Tangier one seems to have embarked on a petrified ocean in a boat hardly equal to the adventure. Then, as one leaps and plunges over humps and ruts, down sheer banks into rivers, and up precipices into sand-pits, one gradually gains faith in one's conveyance and in one's spinal column; but both must be sound in every joint to resist the strain of the long miles to Arbaoua, the frontier post of the French protectorate.

Luckily there are other things to think about. At the first turn out of Tangier, Europe and the European disappear, and as soon as the motor begins to dip and rise over the arid little hills beyond to the last gardens one is sure that every figure on the road will be picturesque instead of prosaic, every garment graceful instead of grotesque. One

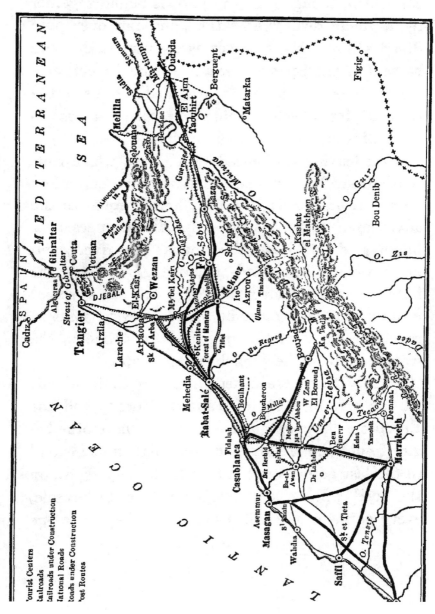

The part of Morocco visited by Mrs Wharton

knows, too, that there will be no more omnibuses
or trams or motorcyclists, but only long lines of
camels rising up in brown friezes against the sky,
little black donkeys trotting across the scrub under
bulging pack-saddles, and noble draped figures
walking beside them or majestically perching on
their rumps. And for miles and miles there will
be no more towns—only, at intervals on the naked
slopes, circles of rush-roofed huts in a blue stock-
ade of cactus, or a hundred or two nomad tents of
black camel's hair resting on walls of wattled thorn
and grouped about a terebinth-tree and a well.

Between these nomad colonies lies the *bled*, the
immense waste of fallow land and palmetto desert:
an earth as void of life as the sky above it of clouds.
The scenery is always the same; but if one has the
love of great emptinesses, and of the play of light on
long stretches of parched earth and rock, the same-
ness is part of the enchantment. In such a scene
every landmark takes on an extreme value. For
miles one watches the little white dome of a saint's
grave rising and disappearing with the undulations
of the trail; at last one is abreast of it, and the
solitary tomb, alone with its fig-tree and its broken

well-curb, puts a meaning into the waste. The same importance, but intensified, marks the appearance of every human figure. The two white-draped riders passing single file up the red slope to that ring of tents on the ridge have a mysterious and inexplicable importance: one follows their progress with eyes that ache with conjecture. More exciting still is the encounter of the first veiled woman heading a little cavalcade from the south. All the mystery that awaits us looks out through the eye-slits in the grave-clothes muffling her. Where have they come from, where are they going, all these slow wayfarers out of the unknown? Probably only from one thatched *douar** to another; but interminable distances unroll behind them, they breathe of Timbuctoo and the farthest desert. Just such figures must swarm in the Saharan cities, in the Soudan and Senegal. There is no break in the links: these wanderers have looked on at the building of cities that were dust when the Romans pushed their outposts across the Atlas.

* Village of tents. The village of mud-huts is called a *nourwal*.

III

EL-KSAR TO RABAT

A TOWN at last—its nearness announced by the multiplied ruts of the trail, the cactus hedges, the fig-trees weighed down by dust leaning over ruinous earthern walls. And here are the first houses of the European El-Ksar—neat white Spanish houses on the slope outside the old Arab settlement. Of the Arab town itself, above reed stockades and brown walls, only a minaret and a few flat roofs are visible. Under the walls drowse the usual gregarious Lazaruses; others, temporarily resuscitated, trail their grave-clothes after a line of camels and donkeys toward the olive-gardens outside the town.

The way to Rabat is long and difficult, and there is no time to visit El-Ksar, though its minaret beckons so alluringly above the fruit-orchards; so we stop for luncheon outside the walls, at a canteen with a corrugated iron roof where skinny Spaniards are serving thick purple wine and eggs fried in oil to a party of French soldiers. The heat has suddenly become intolerable, and a flaming wind straight from the south brings in at the door, with a cloud of blue flies, the smell of camels and trampled herbs and the strong spices of the bazaars.

Luncheon over, we hurry on between the cactus hedges, and then plunge back into the waste. Beyond El-Ksar the last hills of the Rif die away, and there is a stretch of wilderness without an outline till the Lesser Atlas begins to rise in the east. Once in the French protectorate the trail improves, but there are still difficult bits; and finally, on a high plateau, the chauffeur stops in a web of crisscross trails, throws up his hands, and confesses that he has lost his way. The heat is mortal at the moment. For the last hour the red breath of the sirocco has risen from every hollow into which we dipped; now it hangs about us in the open, as if we had caught it in our wheels and it had to pause above us when we paused.

All around is the featureless wild land, palmetto scrub stretching away into eternity. A few yards off rises the inevitable ruined *koubba** with its fig-tree: in the shade under its crumbling wall the buzz of the flies is like the sound of frying. Farther off,

* Saint's tomb. The saint himself is called a *marabout*.

[12]

we discern a cluster of huts, and presently some Arab boys and a tall pensive shepherd come hurrying across the scrub. They are full of good-will, and no doubt of information; but our chauffeur speaks no Arabic and the talk dies down into shrugs and head-shakings. The Arabs retire to the shade of the wall, and we decide to start—for anywhere . . .

The chauffeur turns the crank, but there is no responding quiver. Something has gone wrong; we can't move, and it is not much comfort to remember that, if we could, we should not know where to go. At least we should be cooler in motion than sitting still under the blinding sky.

Such an adventure initiates one at the outset into the stern facts of desert motoring. Every detail of our trip from Tangier to Rabat had been carefully planned to keep us in unbroken contact with civilization. We were to "tub" in one European hotel, and to dine in another, with just enough picnicking between to give a touch of local colour. But let one little cog slip and the whole plan falls to bits, and we are alone in the old untamed Moghreb, as remote from Europe as any mediæval adventurer. If one lose one's way in

Morocco, civilization vanishes as though it were a magic carpet rolled up by a Djinn.

It is a good thing to begin with such a mishap, not only because it develops the fatalism necessary to the enjoyment of Africa, but because it lets one at once into the mysterious heart of the country: a country so deeply conditioned by its miles and miles of uncitied wilderness that until one has known the wilderness one cannot begin to understand the cities.

We came to one at length, after sunset on that first endless day. The motor, cleverly patched up, had found its way to a real road, and speeding along between the stunted cork-trees of the forest of Mamora brought us to a last rise from which we beheld in the dusk a line of yellow walls backed by the misty blue of the Atlantic. Salé, the fierce old pirate town, where Robinson Crusoe was so long a slave, lay before us, snow-white in its cheese-coloured ramparts skirted by fig and olive gardens. Below its gates a stretch of waste land, endlessly trailed over by mules and camels, sloped down to the mouth of the Bou-Regreg, the blue-brown river dividing it from Rabat. The motor stopped at the landing-stage of the steam-ferry; crowding about it were droves of donkeys, knots of camels, plump-faced merchants on crimson-saddled mules, with negro servants at their bridles, bare-legged water-carriers with hairy goat-skins slung over their shoulders, and Arab women in a heap of veils, cloaks, mufflings, all of the same ashy white, the caftans of clutched children peeping through in patches of old rose and lilac and pale green.

Across the river the native town of Rabat lay piled up on an orange-red cliff beaten by the Atlantic. Its walls, red too, plunged into the darkening breakers at the mouth of the river; and behind it, stretching up to the mighty tower of Hassan, and the ruins of the Great Mosque, the scattered houses of the European city showed their many lights across the plain.

IV

THE KASBAH OF THE OUDAYAS

SALÉ the white and Rabat the red frown at each other over the foaming bar of the Bou-Regreg, each walled, terraced, minareted, and presenting a singularly complete picture of the two types of Moroccan town, the snowy and the tawny. To the gates of both the Atlantic breakers roll in with the boom of northern seas, and under a misty northern sky. It is one of the surprises of Morocco to find the familiar African pictures bathed in this unfamiliar haze. Even the fierce midday sun does not wholly dispel it: the air remains thick, opalescent, like water slightly clouded by milk. One is tempted to say that Morocco is Tunisia seen by moonlight.

The European town of Rabat, a rapidly developing community, lies almost wholly outside the walls of the old Arab city. The latter, founded in the twelfth century by the great Almohad conqueror of Spain, Yacoub-el-Mansour, stretches its mighty walls to the river's mouth. Thence they climb the cliff to enclose the Kasbah * of the Oudayas, a troublesome tribe whom one of the Almohad Sultans, mistrusting their good faith, packed up one day, flocks, tents and camels, and carried across the *bled* to stow them into these stout walls under his imperial eye. Great crenellated ramparts, cyclopean, superb, follow the curve of the

* Citadel.

From a photograph from the Service des Beaux-Arts au Maroc

Rabat—general view from the Kasbah of the Oudayas

cliff. On the landward side they are interrupted by a gate-tower resting on one of the most nobly decorated of the horseshoe arches that break the mighty walls of Moroccan cities. Underneath the tower the vaulted entrance turns, Arab fashion, at right angles, profiling its red arch against darkness and mystery. This bending of passages, so characteristic a device of the Moroccan builder, is like an architectural expression of the tortuous secret soul of the land.

Outside the Kasbah a narrow foot-path is squeezed between the walls and the edge of the cliff. Toward sunset it looks down on a strange scene. To the south of the citadel the cliff descends to a long dune sloping to a sand-beach; and dune and beach are covered with the slanting headstones of the immense Arab cemetery of El Alou. Acres and acres of graves fall away from the red ramparts to the grey sea; and breakers rolling straight from America send their spray across the lowest stones.

There are always things going on toward evening in an Arab cemetery. In this one, travellers from the *bled* are camping in one corner, donkeys grazing (on heaven knows what), a camel dozing under its pack; in another, about a new-made grave, there are ritual movements of muffled figures and wailings of a funeral hymn half drowned by the waves. Near us, on a fallen headstone, a man with a thoughtful face sits chatting with two friends and hugging to his breast a tiny boy who looks like a grasshopper in his green caftan; a little way off, a solitary philosopher, his eye fixed on the sunset, lies on another grave, smoking his long pipe of kif.

There is infinite sadness in this scene under the fading sky, beside the cold welter of the Atlantic. One seems to be not in Africa itself, but in the Africa that northern crusaders may have dreamed of in snow-bound castles by colder shores of the same ocean. This is what Moghreb must have looked like to the confused imagination of the Middle Ages, to Norman knights burning to ransom the Holy Places, or Hansa merchants devising, in steep-roofed towns, of Barbary and the long caravans bringing apes and gold-powder from the south.

Inside the gate of the Kasbah one comes on more waste land and on other walls—for all Moroccan towns are enclosed in circuit within circuit of battlemented masonry. Then, unexpectedly, a gate in one of the inner walls lets one into a tiled court enclosed in a traceried cloister and overlooking an orange-grove that rises out of a carpet of roses. This peaceful and well-ordered place is the interior of the Medersa (the college) of the Oudayas. Morocco is full of these colleges, or rather lodging-houses of the students frequenting the mosques; for all Mahometan education is given in the mosque itself, only the preparatory work being done in the colleges. The most beautiful of the Medersas date from the earlier years of the long Merinid dynasty (1248–1548), the period at which Moroccan art, freed from too distinctively Spanish and Arab influences, began to develop a delicate grace of its own as far removed from the extravagance of Spanish ornament as from the inheritance of Roman-Byzantine motives that the first Moslem invasion had brought with it from Syria and Mesopotamia.

These exquisite collegiate buildings, though still in use whenever they are near a well-known mosque, have all fallen into a state of sordid disrepair. The

Moroccan Arab, though he continues to build—
and fortunately to build in the old tradition, which
has never been lost—has, like all Orientals, an in-
vincible repugnance to repairing and restoring, and
one after another the frail exposed Arab structures,
with their open courts and badly constructed
terrace-roofs, are crumbling into ruin. Happily the
French Government has at last been asked to in-
tervene, and all over Morocco the Medersas are
being repaired with skill and discretion. That of
the Oudayas is already completely restored, and
as it had long fallen into disuse it has been trans-
formed by the Ministry of Fine Arts into a museum
of Moroccan art.

The plan of the Medersas is always much the
same: the eternal plan of the Arab house, built
about one or more arcaded courts, with long narrow rooms enclosing them on the ground floor, and
several stories above, reached by narrow stairs, and
often opening on finely carved cedar galleries.
The chief difference between the Medersa and the
private house, or even the *fondak*,* lies in the use to
which the rooms are put. In the Medersas, one

* The Moroccan inn or caravanserai.

Rabat—interior court of the Medersa of the Oudayas

of the ground-floor apartments is always fitted up as a chapel, and shut off from the court by carved cedar doors still often touched with old gilding and vermilion. There are always a few students praying in the chapel, while others sit in the doors of the upper rooms, their books on their knees, or lean over the carved galleries chatting with their companions who are washing their feet at the marble fountain in the court, preparatory to entering the chapel.

In the Medersa of the Oudayas, these native activities have been replaced by the lifeless hush of a museum. The rooms are furnished with old rugs, pottery, brasses, the curious embroidered hangings which line the tents of the chiefs, and other specimens of Arab art. One room reproduces a barber's shop in the bazaar, its benches covered with fine matting, the hanging mirror inlaid with mother-of-pearl, the razor-handles of silver *niello*. The horseshoe arches of the outer gallery look out on orange-blossoms, roses and the sea. It is all beautiful, calm and harmonious; and if one is tempted to mourn the absence of life and local colour, one has only to visit an abandoned

Medersa to see that, but for French intervention,
the charming colonnades and cedar chambers of
the college of the Oudayas would by this time be a
heap of undistinguished rubbish—for plaster and
rubble do not "die in beauty" like the firm stones
of Rome.

V

ROBINSON CRUSOE'S "SALLEE"

BEFORE Morocco passed under the rule of the
great governor who now administers it, the European colonists made short work of the beauty
and privacy of the old Arab towns in which they
established themselves.

On the west coast, especially, where the Mediterranean peoples, from the Phenicians to the Portuguese, have had trading-posts for over two thousand
years, the harm done to such seaboard towns as
Tangier, Rabat and Casablanca is hard to estimate.
The modern European colonist apparently imagined that to plant his warehouses, *cafés* and cinema-
palaces within the walls which for so long had
fiercely excluded him was the most impressive way
of proclaiming his domination.

Under General Lyautey such views are no longer tolerated. Respect for native habits, native beliefs and native architecture is the first principle inculcated in the civil servants attached to his administration. Not only does he require that the native towns shall be kept intact, and no European building erected within them; a sense of beauty not often vouchsafed to Colonial governors causes him to place the administration buildings so far beyond the walls that the modern colony grouped around them remains entirely distinct from the old town, instead of growing out of it like an ugly excrescence.

The Arab quarter of Rabat was already irreparably disfigured when General Lyautey came to Morocco; but ferocious old Salé, Phenician counting-house and breeder of Barbary pirates, had been saved from profanation by its Moslem fanaticism. Few Christian feet had entered its walls except those of the prisoners who, like Robinson Crusoe, slaved for the wealthy merchants in its mysterious terraced houses. Not till two or three years ago was it completely pacified; and when it opened its gates to the infidel it was still, as it is to-day, the type of the untouched Moroccan city—so untouched that, with the sunlight irradiating its cream-coloured walls and the blue-white domes above them, it rests on its carpet of rich fruit-gardens like some rare specimen of Arab art on a strip of old Oriental velvet.

Within the walls, the magic persists: which does not always happen when one penetrates into the mirage-like cities of Arabian Africa. Salé has the charm of extreme compactness. Crowded between the river-mouth and the sea, its white and pale-blue houses almost touch across the narrow streets, and the reed-thatched bazaars seem like miniature reductions of the great trading labyrinths of Tunis or Fez.

Everything that the reader of the Arabian Nights expects to find is here: the whitewashed niches wherein pale youths sit weaving the fine mattings for which the town is still famous; the tunnelled passages where indolent merchants with bare feet crouch in their little kennels hung with richly or-namented saddlery and arms, or with slippers of pale citron leather and bright embroidered *babouches;* the stalls with fruit, olives, tunny-fish,

From a photograph from the Service des Beaux-Arts au Maroc

Salé—entrance of the Medersa

vague syrupy sweets, candles for saints' tombs, Mantegnesque garlands of red and green peppers, griddle-cakes sizzling on red-hot pans, and all the varied wares and cakes and condiments that the lady in the tale of the Three Calanders went out to buy, that memorable morning in the market of Bagdad.

Only at Salé all is on a small scale: there is not much of any one thing, except of the exquisite matting. The tide of commerce has ebbed from the intractable old city, and one feels, as one watches the listless purchasers in her little languishing bazaars, that her long animosity against the intruder has ended by destroying her own life.

The feeling increases when one leaves the bazaar for the streets adjoining it. An even deeper hush than that which hangs over the well-to-do quarters of all Arab towns broods over these silent thoroughfares, with heavy-nailed doors barring half-ruined houses. In a steep deserted square one of these doors opens its panels of weather-silvered cedar on the court of the frailest, ghostliest of Medersas— mere carved and painted shell of a dead house of learning. Mystic interweavings of endless lines, patient patterns interminably repeated in wood and stone and clay, all are here, from the tessellated paving of the court to the honeycombing of the cedar roof through which a patch of sky shows here and there like an inset of turquoise tiling.

This lovely ruin is in the safe hands of the French Fine Arts administration, and soon the wood-carvers and stucco-workers of Fez will have revived its old perfection; but it will never again be more than a show-Medersa, standing empty and unused beside the mosque behind whose guarded doors and high walls one guesses that the old religious fanaticism of Salé is dying also, as her learning and her commerce have died.

In truth the only life in her is centred in the market-place outside the walls, where big expanding Rabat goes on certain days to provision herself. The market of Salé, though typical of all Moroccan markets, has an animation and picturesqueness of its own. Its rows of white tents pitched on a dusty square between the outer walls and the fruit-gardens make it look as though a hostile tribe had sat down to lay siege to the town; but the army is an army of hucksters, of farmers from the

From a photograph by Schmitt, Rabat

Salé—market-place outside the town

rich black lands along the river, of swarthy nomads and leather-gaitered peasant women from the hills, of slaves and servants and tradesmen from Rabat and Salé; a draped, veiled, turbaned mob shrieking, bargaining, fist-shaking, call on Allah to witness the monstrous villanies of the misbegotten miscreants they are trading with, and then, struck with the mysterious Eastern apathy, sinking down in languid heaps of muslin among the black figs, purple onions and rosy melons, the fluttering hens, the tethered goats, the whinnying foals, that are all enclosed in an outer circle of folded-up camels and of mules dozing under faded crimson saddles.

VI

CHELLA AND THE GREAT MOSQUE

THE Merinid Sultans of Rabat had a terribly troublesome neighbour across the Bou-Regreg, and they built Chella to keep an eye on the pirates of Salé. But Chella has fallen like a Babylonian city triumphed over by the prophets; while Salé, sly, fierce and irrepressible, continued till well on in the nineteenth century to breed pirates and fanatics.

The ruins of Chella lie on the farther side of the plateau above the native town of Rabat. The mighty wall enclosing them faces the city wall of Rabat, looking at it across one of those great red powdery wastes which seem, in this strange land, like death and the desert forever creeping up to overwhelm the puny works of man.

The red waste is scored by countless trains of donkeys carrying water from the springs of Chella, by long caravans of mules and camels, and by the busy motors of the French administration; yet there emanates from it an impression of solitude and decay which even the prosaic tinkle of the trams jogging out from the European town to the Exhibition grounds above the sea cannot long dispel.

Perpetually, even in the new thriving French Morocco, the outline of a ruin or the look in a pair of eyes shifts the scene, rends the thin veil of the European Illusion, and confronts one with the old grey Moslem reality. Passing under the gate of Chella, with its richly carved corbels and lofty crenellated towers, one feels one's self thus completely reabsorbed into the past.

Below the gate the ground slopes away, bare

and blazing, to a hollow where a little blue-green minaret gleams through fig-trees, and fragments of arch and vaulting reveal the outline of a ruined mosque.

Was ever shade so blue-black and delicious as that of the cork-tree near the spring where the donkey's water-cans are being filled? Under its branches a black man in a blue shirt lies immovably sleeping in the dust. Close by women and children splash and chatter about the spring, and the dome of a saint's tomb shines through lustreless leaves. The black man, the donkeys, the women and children, the saint's dome, are all part of the inimitable Eastern scene in which inertia and agitation are so curiously combined, and a surface of shrill noise flickers over depths of such unfathomable silence.

The ruins of Chella belong to the purest period of Moroccan art. The tracery of the broken arches is all carved in stone or in glazed turquoise tiling, and the fragments of wall and vaulting have the firm elegance of a classic ruin. But what would even their beauty be without the leafy setting of the place? The "unimaginable touch of Time" gives Chella its peculiar charm: the aged fig-tree clamped in uptorn tiles and thrusting gouty arms between the arches; the garlanding of vines flung from column to column; the secret pool to which childless women are brought to bathe, and where the tree springing from a cleft of the steps is always hung with the bright bits of stuff which are the votive offerings of Africa.

The shade, the sound of springs, the terraced orange-garden with irises blooming along channels of running water, all this greenery and coolness in the hollow of a fierce red hill make Chella seem, to the traveller new to Africa, the very type and embodiment of its old contrasts of heat and freshness, of fire and languor. It is like a desert traveller's dream in his last fever.

Yacoub-el-Mansour was the fourth of the great Almohad Sultans who, in the twelfth century, drove out the effete Almoravids, and swept their victorious armies from Marrakech to Tunis and from Tangier to Madrid. His grandfather, Abd-el-Moumen, had been occupied with conquest and civic administration. It was said of his rule that "he seized northern Africa to make order prevail

From a photograph from the Service des Beaux-Arts au Maroc

Chella—ruins of mosque

there"; and in fact, out of a welter of wild tribes confusedly fighting and robbing he drew an empire firmly seated and securely governed, wherein caravans travelled from the Atlas to the Straits without fear of attack, and "a soldier wandering through the fields would not have dared to pluck an ear of wheat."

His grandson, the great El-Mansour, was a conqueror too; but where he conquered he planted the undying seed of beauty. The victor of Alarcos, the soldier who subdued the north of Spain, dreamed a great dream of art. His ambition was to bestow on his three capitals, Seville, Rabat and Marrakech, the three most beautiful towers the world had ever seen; and if the tower of Rabat had been completed, and that of Seville had not been injured by Spanish embellishments, his dream would have been realized.

The "Tower of Hassan," as the Sultan's tower is called, rises from the plateau above old Rabat, overlooking the steep cliff that drops down to the last winding of the Bou-Regreg. Truncated at half its height, it stands on the edge of the cliff, a far-off beacon to travellers by land and sea. It is

one of the world's great monuments, so sufficient
in strength and majesty that until one has seen its
fellow, the Koutoubya of Marrakech, one wonders
if the genius of the builder could have carried such
perfect balance of massive wall-spaces and traceried
openings to a triumphant completion.

Near the tower, the red-brown walls and huge
piers of the mosque built at the same time stretch
their roofless alignment beneath the sky. This
mosque, before it was destroyed, must have been
one of the finest monuments of Almohad architecture in Morocco: now, with its tumbled red masses
of masonry and vast cisterns overhung by clumps
of blue aloes, it still forms a ruin of Roman grandeur.

The Mosque, the Tower, the citadel of the
Oudayas, and the mighty walls and towers of
Chella, compose an architectural group as noble
and complete as that of some mediæval Tuscan
city. All they need to make the comparison exact
is that they should have been compactly massed
on a steep hill, instead of lying scattered over the
wide spaces between the promontory of the Oudayas and the hill-side of Chella.

The founder of Rabat, the great Yacoub-el-

Mansour, called it, in memory of the battle of Alarcos, "The Camp of Victory" (*Ribat-el-Path*), and the monuments he bestowed on it justified the name in another sense, by giving it the beauty that lives when battles are forgotten.

II

VOLUBILIS, MOULAY IDRISS AND MEKNEZ

VOLUBILIS, MOULAY IDRISS AND MEKNEZ

I

VOLUBILIS

ONE day before sunrise we set out from Rabat for the ruins of Roman Volubilis.

From the ferry of the Bou-Regreg we looked backward on a last vision of orange ramparts under a night-blue sky sprinkled with stars; ahead, over gardens still deep in shadow, the walls of Salé were passing from drab to peach-colour in the eastern glow. Dawn is the romantic hour in Africa. Dirt and dilapidation disappear under a pearly haze, and a breeze from the sea blows away the memory of fetid markets and sordid heaps of humanity. At that hour the old Moroccan cities look like the ivory citadels in a Persian miniature, and the fat shopkeepers riding out to their vegetable-gardens like Princes sallying forth to rescue captive maidens.

Our way led along the highroad from Rabat to the modern port of Kenitra, near the ruins of the Phenician colony of Mehedyia. Just north of Kenitra we struck the trail, branching off eastward to a European village on the light railway between Rabat and Fez, and beyond the railway-sheds and flat-roofed stores the wilderness began, stretching away into clear distances bounded by the hills of the Rarb,* above which the sun was rising.

Range after range these translucent hills rose before us; all around the solitude was complete. Village life, and even tent life, naturally gathers about a river-bank or a spring; and the waste we were crossing was of waterless sand bound together by a loose desert growth. Only an abandoned well-curb here and there cast its blue shadow on the yellow *bled,* or a saint's tomb hung like a bubble between sky and sand. The light had the preternatural purity which gives a foretaste of mirage: it was the light in which magic becomes real, and which helps to understand how, to people living in

* The high plateau-and-hill formation between Tangier and Fez.

such an atmosphere, the boundary between fact and dream perpetually fluctuates.

The sand was scored with tracks and ruts innumerable, for the road between Rabat and Fez is travelled not only by French government motors but by native caravans and trains of pilgrims to and from the sacred city of Moulay Idriss, the founder of the Idrissite dynasty, whose tomb is in the Zerhoun, the mountain ridge above Volubilis. To untrained eyes it was impossible to guess which of the trails one ought to follow; and without much surprise we suddenly found the motor stopping, while its wheels spun round vainly in the loose sand.

The military chauffeur was not surprised either; nor was Captain de M., the French staff-officer who accompanied us.

"It often happens just here," they admitted philosophically. "When the General goes to Meknez he is always followed by a number of motors, so that if his own is stuck he may go on in another."

This was interesting to know, but not particularly helpful, as the General and his motors were not travelling our way that morning. Nor was any one else, apparently. It is curious how

quickly the *bled* empties itself to the horizon if one
happens to have an accident in it! But we had
learned our lesson between Tangier and Rabat, and
were able to produce a fair imitation of the fatal-
istic smile of the country.

The officer remarked cheerfully that somebody
might turn up, and we all sat down in the *bled*.

A Berber woman, cropping up from nowhere,
came and sat beside us. She had the thin sun-
tanned face of her kind, brilliant eyes touched with
khol, high cheek-bones, and the exceedingly short
upper lip which gives such charm to the smile of
the young nomad women. Her dress was the usual
faded cotton shift, hooked on the shoulders with
brass or silver clasps (still the antique *fibulæ*), and
wound about with a vague drapery in whose folds
a brown baby wriggled.

The coolness of dawn had vanished and the sun
beat down from a fierce sky. The village on the
railway was too far off to be reached on foot, and
there were probably no mules there to spare.
Nearer at hand there was no sign of help: not a
fortified farm, or even a circle of nomad tents. It
was the unadulterated desert—and we waited.

Not in vain; for after an hour or two, from far off in the direction of the hills, there appeared an army with banners. We stared at it unbelievingly. The *mirage*, of course! We were too sophisticated to doubt it, and tales of sun-dazed travellers mocked by such visions rose in our well-stocked memories.

The chauffeur thought otherwise. "Good! That's a pilgrimage from the mountains. They're going to Salé to pray at the tomb of the *marabout;* to-day is his feast-day."

And so they were! And as we hung on their approach, and speculated as to the chances of their stopping to help, I had time to note the beauty of this long train winding toward us under particolored banners. There was something celestial, almost diaphanous, in the hundreds of figures turbaned and draped in white, marching slowly through the hot colorless radiance over the hot colorless sand.

The most part were on foot, or bestriding tiny donkeys, but a stately Caïd rode alone at the end of the line on a horse saddled with crimson velvet; and to him our officer appealed.

The Caïd courteously responded, and twenty or thirty pilgrims were ordered to harness themselves to the motor and haul it back to the trail, while the rest of the procession moved hieratically onward.

I felt scruples at turning from their path even a fraction of this pious company; but they fell to with a saintly readiness, and before long the motor was on the trail. Then rewards were dispensed; and instantly those holy men became a prey to the darkest passions. Even in this land of contrasts the transition from pious serenity to rapacious rage can seldom have been more rapid. The devotees of the *marabout* fought, screamed, tore their garments and rolled over each other with sanguinary gestures in the struggle for our pesetas; then, perceiving our indifference, they suddenly remembered their religious duties, scrambled to their feet, tucked up their flying draperies, and raced after the tail-end of the procession.

Through a golden heat-haze we struggled on to the hills. The country was fallow, and in great part too sandy for agriculture; but here and there we came on one of the deep-set Moroccan rivers,

[42]

with a reddish-yellow course channelled between perpendicular banks of red earth, and marked by a thin line of verdure that widened to fruit-gardens wherever a village had sprung up. We traversed several of these "sedentary" * villages, *nourwals* of clay houses with thatched conical roofs, in gardens of fig, apricot and pomegranate that must be so many pink and white paradises after the winter rains.

One of these villages seemed to be inhabited entirely by blacks, big friendly creatures who came out to tell us by which trail to reach the bridge over the yellow *oued*. In the *oued* their womenkind were washing the variegated family rags. They were handsome blue-bronze creatures, bare to the waist, with tight black astrakhan curls and firmly sculptured legs and ankles; and all around them, like a swarm of gnats, danced countless jolly pickaninnies, naked as lizards, with the spindle legs and globular stomachs of children fed only on cereals.

Half terrified but wholly interested, these in-

* So called to distinguish them from the tent villages of the less settled groups.

fants buzzed about the motor while we stopped to photograph them; and as we watched their antics we wondered whether they were the descendants of the little Soudanese boys whom the founder of Meknez, the terrible Sultan Moulay-Ismaël, used to carry off from beyond the Atlas and bring up in his military camps to form the nucleus of the Black Guard which defended his frontiers. We were on the line of travel between Meknez and the sea, and it seemed not unlikely that these *nourwals* were all that remained of scattered outposts of Moulay-Ismaël's legionaries.

After a time we left *oueds* and villages behind us and were in the mountains of the Rarb, toiling across a high sandy plateau. Far off a fringe of vegetation showed promise of shade and water, and at last, against a pale mass of olive-trees, we saw the sight which, at whatever end of the world one comes upon it, wakes the same sense of awe: the ruin of a Roman city.

Volubilis (called by the Arabs the Castle of the Pharaohs) is the only considerable Roman colony so far discovered in Morocco. It stands on the extreme ledge of a high plateau backed by the mountains of the Zerhoun. Below the plateau, the land drops down precipitately to a narrow river-valley green with orchards and gardens, and in the neck of the valley, where the hills meet again, the conical white town of Moulay Idriss, the Sacred City of Morocco, rises sharply against a wooded background.

So the two dominations look at each other across the valley: one, the lifeless Roman ruin, representing a system, an order, a social conception that still run through all our modern ways; the other, the untouched Moslem city, more dead and sucked back into an unintelligible past than any broken architrave of Greece or Rome.

Volubilis seems to have had the extent and wealth of a great military outpost, such as Timgad in Algeria; but in the seventeenth century it was very nearly destroyed by Moulay-Ismaël, the Sultan of the Black Guard, who carried off its monuments piece-meal to build his new capital of Meknez, that Mequinez of contemporary travellers which was held to be one of the wonders of the age.

Little remains to Volubilis in the way of important monuments: only the fragments of a basilica, part of an arch of triumph erected in honour of Caracalla, and the fallen columns and architraves which strew the path of Rome across the world. But its site is magnificent; and as the excavation of the ruins was interrupted by the war it is possible that subsequent search may bring forth other treasures comparable to the beautiful bronze *sloughi* (the African hound) which is now its principal possession.

It was delicious, after seven hours of travel under the African sun, to sit on the shady terrace where the Curator of Volubilis, M. Louis Châtelain, welcomes his visitors. The French Fine Arts have built a charming house with gardens and pergolas for the custodian of the ruins, and have found in M. Châtelain an archæologist so absorbed in his task that, as soon as conditions permit, every inch of soil in the circumference of the city will be made to yield up whatever secrets it hides.

II

MOULAY IDRISS

WE lingered under the pergolas of Volubilis till the heat grew less intolerable, and then our companions suggested a visit to Moulay Idriss.

From a photograph from the Service des Beaux-Arts au Maroc

Volubilis—the western portico of the basilica of Antonius Pius

Such a possibility had not occurred to us, and even Captain de M. seemed to doubt whether the expedition were advisable. Moulay Idriss was still said to be resentful of Christian intrusion: it was only a year before that the first French officers had entered it.

But M. Châtelain was confident that there would be no opposition to our visit, and with the piled-up terraces and towers of the Sacred City growing golden in the afternoon light across the valley it was impossible to hesitate.

We drove down through an olive-wood as ancient as those of Mitylene and Corfu, and then along the narrowing valley, between gardens luxuriant even in the parched Moroccan autumn. Presently the motor began to climb the steep road to the town, and at a gateway we got out and were met by the native chief of police. Instantly at the high windows of mysterious houses veiled heads appeared and sidelong eyes cautiously inspected us. But the quarter was deserted, and we walked on without meeting any one to the Street of the Weavers, a silent narrow way between low whitewashed niches like the cubicles in a convent. In each niche sat a grave white-robed youth, forming a great amphora-shaped grain-basket out of closely plaited straw. Vine-leaves and tendrils hung through the reed roofing overhead, and grape-clusters cast their classic shadow at our feet. It was like walking on the unrolled frieze of a white Etruscan vase patterned with black vine garlands.

The silence and emptiness of the place began to strike us: there was no sign of the Oriental crowd that usually springs out of the dust at the approach of strangers. But suddenly we heard close by the lament of the *rekka* (a kind of long fife), accompanied by a wild thrum-thrum of earthenware drums and a curious excited chanting of men's voices. I had heard such a chant before, at the other end of North Africa, in Kairouan, one of the other great Sanctuaries of Islam, where the sect of the Aïssaouas celebrate their sanguinary rites in the *Zaouïa** of their confraternity. Yet it seemed incredible that if the Aïssaouas of Moulay Idriss were performing their ceremonies that day the chief of police should be placidly leading us through the streets in the very direction from which the

* Sacred college.

[48]

Moulay-Idriss (9,000 inhabitants)

chant was coming. The Moroccan, though he has no desire to get into trouble with the Christian, prefers to be left alone on feast-days, especially in such a stronghold of the faith as Moulay Idriss.

But "Geschehen ist geschehen" is the sum of Oriental philosophy. For centuries Moulay Idriss had held out fanatically on its holy steep; then, suddenly, in 1916, its chiefs saw that the game was up, and surrendered without a pretense of resistance. Now the whole thing was over, the new conditions were accepted, and the chief of police assured us that with the French uniform at our side we should be safe anywhere.

"The Aïssaouas?" he explained. "No, this is another sect, the Hamadchas, who are performing their ritual dance on the feast-day of their patron, the *marabout* Hamadch, whose tomb is in the Zerhoun. The feast is celebrated publicly in the market-place of Moulay Idriss."

As he spoke we came out into the market-place, and understood why there had been no crowd at the gate. All the population was in the square and on the roofs that mount above it, tier by tier, against the wooded hillside: Moulay Idriss had better to do that day than to gape at a few tourists in dust-coats.

Short of Sfax, and the other coast cities of eastern Tunisia, there is surely not another town in North Africa as white as Moulay Idriss. Some are pale blue and pinky yellow, like the Kasbah of Tangier, or cream and blue like Salé; but Tangier and Salé, for centuries continuously subject to European influences, have probably borrowed their colors from Genoa and the Italian Riviera. In the interior of the country, and especially in Morocco, where the whole color-scheme is much soberer than in Algeria and Tunisia, the color of the native houses is always a penitential shade of mud and ashes.

But Moulay Idriss, that afternoon, was as white as if its arcaded square had been scooped out of a big cream cheese. The late sunlight lay like gold-leaf on one side of the square, the other was in pure blue shade; and above it, the crowded roofs, terraces and balconies packed with women in bright dresses looked like a flower-field on the edge of a marble quarry.

The bright dresses were as unusual a sight as the white walls, for the average Moroccan crowd

From a photograph from the Service des Beaux-Arts au Maroc

Moulay-Idriss—the market-place

is the color of its houses. But the occasion was a special one, for these feasts of the Hamadchas occur only twice a year, in spring and autumn, and as the ritual dances take place out of doors, instead of being performed inside the building of the confraternity, the feminine population seizes the opportunity to burst into flower on the housetops.

It is rare, in Morocco, to see in the streets or the bazaars any women except of the humblest classes, household slaves, servants, peasants from the country or small tradesmen's wives; and even they (with the exception of the unveiled Berber women) are wrapped in the prevailing grave-clothes. The *filles de joie* and dancing-girls whose brilliant dresses enliven certain streets of the Algerian and Tunisian towns are invisible, or at least unnoticeable, in Morocco, where life, on the whole, seems so much less gay and brightly-tinted; and the women of the richer classes, mercantile or aristocratic, never leave their harems except to be married or buried. A throng of women dressed in light colors is therefore to be seen in public only when some street festival draws them to the roofs. Even then it is probable that the throng is mostly composed of

slaves, household servants, and women of the lower
bourgeoisie; but as they are all dressed in mauve
and rose and pale green, with long earrings and
jewelled head-bands flashing through their parted
veils, the illusion, from a little distance, is as complete as though they were the ladies in waiting of
the Queen of Sheba; and that radiant afternoon at
Moulay Idriss, above the vine-garlanded square,
and against the background of piled-up terraces,
their vivid groups were in such contrast to the usual
gray assemblages of the East that the scene seemed
like a setting for some extravagantly staged ballet.

For the same reason the spectacle unrolling itself
below us took on a blessed air of unreality. Any
normal person who has seen a dance of the Aïssaouas
and watched them swallow thorns and hot coals,
slash themselves with knives, and roll on the floor
in epilepsy must have privately longed, after the
first excitement was over, to fly from the repulsive
scene. The Hamadchas are much more savage
than Aïssaouas, and carry much farther their display of cataleptic anæsthesia; and, knowing this, I
had wondered how long I should be able to stand
the sight of what was going on below our terrace.

Moulay-Idriss—market-place on the day of the ritual dance of the Hamadchas

But the beauty of the setting redeemed the bestial horror. In that unreal golden light the scene became merely symbolical: it was like one of those strange animal masks which the Middle Ages brought down from antiquity by way of the satyr-plays of Greece, and of which the half-human protagonists still grin and contort themselves among the Christian symbols of Gothic cathedrals.

At one end of the square the musicians stood on a stone platform above the dancers. Like the musicians in a bas-relief they were flattened side by side against a wall, the fife-players with lifted arms and inflated cheeks, the drummers pounding frantically on long earthenware drums shaped like enormous hour-glasses and painted in barbaric patterns; and below, down the length of the market-place, the dance unrolled itself in a frenzied order that would have filled with envy a Paris or London impresario.

In its centre an inspired-looking creature whirled about on his axis, the black ringlets standing out in snaky spirals from his haggard head, his cheek-muscles convulsively twitching. Around him, but a long way off, the dancers rocked and circled with

long raucous cries dominated by the sobbing boom-
ing music; and in the sunlit space between dancers
and holy man, two or three impish children bobbed
about with fixed eyes and a grimace of comic
frenzy, solemnly parodying his contortions.

Meanwhile a tall grave personage in a doge-like
cap, the only calm figure in the tumult, moved
gravely here and there, regulating the dance, stimu-
lating the frenzy, or calming some devotee who had
broken the ranks and lay tossing and foaming on
the stones. There was something far more sinister
in this passionless figure, holding his hand on the
key that let loose such crazy forces, than in the
poor central whirligig who merely set the rhythm
of the convulsions.

The dancers were all dressed in white caftans
or in the blue shirts of the lowest classes. In the
sunlight something that looked like fresh red paint
glistened on their shaved black or yellow skulls and
made dark blotches on their garments. At first
these stripes and stains suggested only a gaudy
ritual ornament like the pattern on the drums;
then one saw that the paint, or whatever it was,
kept dripping down from the whirling caftans and

forming fresh pools among the stones; that as one of the pools dried up another formed, redder and more glistening, and that these pools were fed from great gashes which the dancers hacked in their own skulls and breasts with hatchets and sharpened stones. The dance was a blood-rite, a great sacrificial symbol, in which blood flowed so freely that all the rocking feet were splashed with it.

Gradually, however, it became evident that many of the dancers simply rocked and howled, without hacking themselves, and that most of the bleeding skulls and breasts belonged to negroes. Every now and then the circle widened to let in another figure, black or dark yellow, the figure of some humble blue-shirted spectator suddenly "getting religion" and rushing forward to snatch a weapon and baptize himself with his own blood; and as each new recruit joined the dancers the music shrieked louder and the devotees howled more wolfishly. And still, in the centre, the mad *marabout* spun, and the children bobbed and mimicked him and rolled their diamond eyes.

Such is the dance of the Hamadchas, of the confraternity of the *marabout* Hamadch, a powerful

saint of the seventeenth century, whose tomb is in
the Zerhoun above Moulay Idriss. Hamadch, it
appears, had a faithful slave, who, when his master
died, killed himself in despair, and the self-inflicted
wounds of the brotherhood are supposed to sym-
bolize the slave's suicide; though no doubt the
origin of the ceremony might be traced back to the
depths of that ensanguined grove where Mr. Fraser
plucked the Golden Bough.

The more naïve interpretation, however, has its
advantages, since it enables the devotees to divide
their ritual duties into two classes, the devotions
of the free men being addressed to the saint who
died in his bed, while the slaves belong to the
slave, and must therefore simulate his horrid end.
And this is the reason why most of the white caftans simply rock and writhe, while the humble blue
shirts drip with blood.

The sun was setting when we came down from
our terrace above the market-place. To find a
lodging for the night we had to press on to Meknez, where we were awaited at the French military
post; therefore we were reluctantly obliged to re-
fuse an invitation to take tea with the Caïd, whose
high-perched house commands the whole white

From a photograph taken by Captain Brassard of the French Army   Moulay-Idriss—the market-place.   Procession of the confraternity of the Hamadchas

amphitheatre of the town. It was disappointing to leave Moulay Idriss with the Hamadchas howling their maddest, and so much besides to see; but as we drove away under the long shadows of the olives we counted ourselves lucky to have entered the sacred town, and luckier still to have been there on the day of the dance which, till a year ago, no foreigner had been allowed to see.

A fine French road runs from Moulay Idriss to Meknez, and we flew on through the dusk between wooded hills and open stretches on which the fires of nomad camps put orange splashes in the darkness. Then the moon rose, and by its light we saw a widening valley, and gardens and orchards that stretched up to a great walled city outlined against the stars.

III

MEKNEZ

ALL that evening, from the garden of the Military Subdivision on the opposite height, we sat and looked across at the dark tree-clumps and moonlit walls of Meknez, and listened to its fantastic history.

Meknez was built by the Sultan Moulay-Ismaël,

around the nucleus of a small town of which the site happened to please him, at the very moment when Louis XIV was creating Versailles. The coincidence of two contemporary autocrats calling cities out of the wilderness has caused persons with a taste for analogy to describe Meknez as the Versailles of Morocco: an epithet which is about as instructive as it would be to call Phidias the Benvenuto Cellini of Greece.

There is, however, a pretext for the comparison in the fact that the two sovereigns took a lively interest in each other's affairs. Moulay-Ismaël sent several embassies to treat with Louis XIV on the eternal question of piracy and the ransom of Christian captives, and the two rulers were continually exchanging gifts and compliments.

The governor of Tetouan, who was sent to Paris in 1680, having brought as presents to the French King a lion, a lioness, a tigress, and four ostriches, Louis XIV shortly afterward despatched M. de Saint-Amand to Morocco with two dozen watches, twelve pieces of gold brocade, a cannon six feet long and other firearms. After this the relations between the two courts remained friendly

From a photograph from the Service des Beaux-Arts au Maroc

Meknez—gate: "Bab-Mansour"

till 1693, at which time they were strained by the refusal of France to return the Moorish captives who were employed on the king's galleys, and who were probably as much needed there as the Sultan's Christian slaves for the building of Moorish palaces.

Six years later the Sultan despatched Abdallah-ben-Aïssa to France to reopen negotiations. The ambassador was as brilliantly received and as eagerly run after as a modern statesman on an official mission, and his candidly expressed admiration for the personal charms of the Princesse de Conti, one of the French monarch's legitimatized children, is supposed to have been mistaken by the court for an offer of marriage from the Emperor of Barbary. But he came back without a treaty.

Moulay-Ismaël, whose long reign (1673 to 1727) and extraordinary exploits make him already a legendary figure, conceived, early in his career, a passion for Meknez; and through all his troubled rule, with its alternations of barbaric warfare and far-reaching negotiations, palace intrigue, crazy bloodshed and great administrative reforms, his heart perpetually reverted to the wooded slopes on which he dreamed of building a city more splendid than Fez or Marrakech.

"The Sultan" (writes his chronicler Aboul Kasim-ibn-Ahmad, called "Ezziani") "loved Meknez, the climate of which had enchanted him, and he would have liked never to leave it." He left it, indeed, often, left it perpetually, to fight with revolted tribes in the Atlas, to defeat one Berber army after another, to carry his arms across the High Atlas into the Souss, to adorn Fez with the heads of seven hundred vanquished chiefs, to put down his three rebellious brothers, to strip all the cities of his empire of their negroes and transport them to Meknez ("so that not a negro, man, woman or child, slave or free, was left in any part of the country"); to fight and defeat the Christians (1683); to take Tangier, to conduct a campaign on the Moulouya, to lead the holy war against the Spanish (1689), to take Larache, the Spanish commercial post on the west coast (which furnished eighteen hundred captives for Meknez); to lay siege to Ceuta, conduct a campaign against the Turks of Algiers, repress the pillage in his army, subdue more tribes, and build forts for his

Black Legionaries from Oudjda to the Oued Noun. But almost each year's bloody record ends with the placid phrase: "Then the Sultan returned to Meknez."

In the year 1701, Ezziani writes, the indomitable old man "deprived his rebellious sons of their principalities; after which date he consecrated himself exclusively to the building of his palaces and the planting of his gardens. And in 1720 (nineteen years later in this long reign!) he ordered the destruction of the mausoleum of Moulay Idriss for the purpose of enlarging it. And to gain the necessary space he bought all the adjacent land, and the workmen did not leave these new labors till they were entirely completed."

In this same year there was levied on Fez a new tax which was so heavy that the inhabitants were obliged to abandon the city.

Yet it is written of this terrible old monarch, who devastated whole districts, and sacrificed uncounted thousands of lives for his ruthless pleasure, that under his administration of his chaotic and turbulent empire "the country rejoiced in the most complete security. A Jew or a woman might travel

alone from Oudjda to the Oued Noun without any
one's asking their business. Abundance reigned
throughout the land: grain, food, cattle were to be
bought for the lowest prices. Nowhere in the
whole of Morocco was a highwayman or a robber
to be found."

And probably both sides of the picture are true.

What, then, was the marvel across the valley,
what were the "lordly pleasure-houses" to whose
creation and enlargement Moulay-Ismaël returned
again and again amid the throes and violences of a
nearly centenarian life?

The chronicler continues: "The Sultan caused all
the houses near the Kasbah* to be demolished, *and
compelled the inhabitants to carry away the ruins of
their dwellings.* All the eastern end of the town was
also torn down, and the ramparts were rebuilt. He
also built the Great Mosque next to the palace of
Nasr. . . . He occupied himself personally with
the construction of his palaces, and before one was
finished he caused another to be begun. He built
the mosque of Elakhdar; the walls of the new town

* The citadal of old Meknez.

were pierced with twenty fortified gates and surmounted with platforms for cannon. Within the
walls he made a great artificial lake where one
might row in boats. There was also a granary with
immense subterranean reservoirs of water, and a
stable *three miles long* for the Sultan's horses and
mules; twelve thousand horses could be stabled in
it. The flooring rested on vaults in which the
grain for the horses was stored. . . . He also
built the palace of Elmansour, which had twenty
cupolas; from the top of each cupola one could look
forth on the plain and the mountains around Meknez. All about the stables the rarest trees were
planted. Within the walls were fifty palaces, each
with its own mosque and its baths. Never was
such a thing known in any country, Arab or foreign, pagan or Moslem. The guarding of the doors
of these palaces was intrusted to twelve hundred
black eunuchs."

Such were the wonders that seventeenth century travellers toiled across the desert to see, and
from which they came back dazzled and almost incredulous, as if half-suspecting that some djinn
had deluded them with the vision of a phantom

city. But for the soberer European records, and
the evidence of the ruins themselves (for the whole
of the new Meknez is a ruin), one might indeed be
inclined to regard Ezziani's statements as an Oriental fable; but the briefest glimpse of Moulay-
Ismaël's Meknez makes it easy to believe all his
chronicler tells of it, even to the three miles of
stables.

Next morning we drove across the valley and,
skirting the old town on the hill, entered, by one of
the twenty gates of Moulay-Ismaël, a long empty
street lined with half-ruined arcades. Beyond was
another street of beaten red earth bordered by
high red walls blotched with gray and mauve.
Ahead of us this road stretched out interminably
(Meknez, before Washington, was the "city of
magnificent distances"), and down its empty length
only one or two draped figures passed, like shadows
on the way to Shadowland. It was clear that the
living held no further traffic with the Meknez of
Moulay-Ismaël.

Here it was at last. Another great gateway let
us, under a resplendently bejewelled arch of tur-
quoise-blue and green, into another walled empti-

ness of red clay; a third gate opened into still vaster
vacancies, and at their farther end rose a colossal
red ruin, something like the lower stories of a
Roman amphitheatre that should stretch out in-
definitely instead of forming a circle, or like a
series of Roman aqueducts built side by side and
joined into one structure. Below this indescribable
ruin the arid ground sloped down to an artificial
water which was surely the lake that the Sultan
had made for his boating-parties; and beyond it
more red earth stretched away to more walls and
gates, with glimpses of abandoned palaces and huge
crumbling angle-towers.

The vastness, the silence, the catastrophic desolation of the place, were all the more impressive
because of the relatively recent date of the buildings. As Moulay-Ismaël had dealt with Volubilis,
so time had dealt with his own Meknez; and the
destruction which it had taken thousands of lash-
driven slaves to inflict on the stout walls of the
Roman city, neglect and abandonment had here
rapidly accomplished. But though the sun-baked
clay of which the impatient Sultan built his pleasure-houses will not suffer comparison with the

firm stones of Rome, "the high Roman fashion" is visible in the shape and outline of these ruins. What they are no one knows. In spite of Ezziani's text (written when the place was already partly destroyed) archæologists disagree as to the uses of the crypt of rose-flushed clay whose twenty rows of gigantic arches are so like an alignment of Roman aqueducts. Were these the vaulted granaries, or the subterranean reservoirs under the three miles of stabling which housed the twelve thousand horses? The stables, at any rate, were certainly near this spot, for the lake adjoins the ruins as in the chronicler's description; and between it and old Meknez, behind walls within walls, lie all that remains of the fifty palaces with their cupolas, gardens, mosques and baths.

This inner region is less ruined than the mysterious vaulted structure, and one of the palaces, being still reserved for the present Sultan's use, cannot be visited; but we wandered unchallenged through desert courts, gardens of cypress and olive where dried fountains and painted summer-houses are falling into dust, and barren spaces enclosed in long empty façades. It was all the work of an

[66]

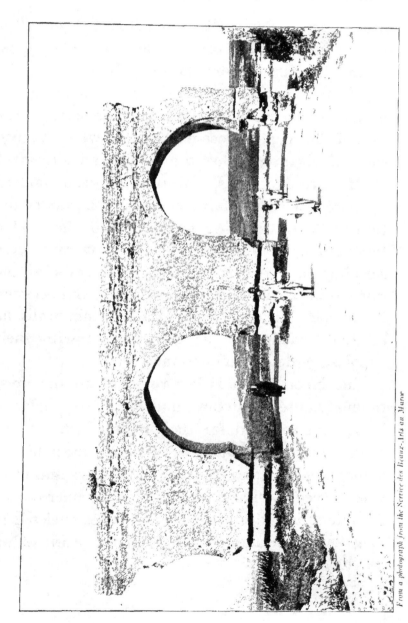

From a photograph from the Service des Beaux-Arts au Maroc

Meknez—the ruins of the palace of Moulay-Ismaël

eager and imperious old man, who, to realize his dream quickly, built in perishable materials; but the design, the dimensions, the whole conception, show that he had not only heard of Versailles but had looked with his own eyes on Volubilis.

To build on such a scale, and finish the work in a single lifetime, even if the materials be malleable and the life a long one, implies a command of human labor that the other Sultan at Versailles must have envied. The imposition of the *corvée* was of course even simpler in Morocco than in France, since the material to draw on was unlimited, provided one could assert one's power over it; and for that purpose Ismaël had his Black Army, the hundred and fifty thousand disciplined legionaries who enabled him to enforce his rule over all the wild country from Algiers to Agadir.

The methods by which this army were raised and increased are worth recounting in Ezziani's words:

"A *taleb** of Marrakech having shown the Sultan a register containing the names of the negroes who had formed part of the army of El-Mansour,

* Learned man.

Moulay-Ismaël ordered his agents to collect all that
remained of these negroes and their children. . . .
He also sent to the tribes of the Beni-Hasen, and
into the mountains, to purchase all the negroes to
be found there. Thus all that were in the whole of
Moghreb were assembled, from the cities and the
countryside, till not one was left, slave or free.

"These negroes were armed and clothed, and
sent to Mechra Erremel (north of Meknez) where
they were ordered to build themselves houses,
plant gardens and remain till their children were
ten years old. Then the Sultan caused all the
children to be brought to him, both boys and
girls. The boys were apprenticed to masons, car-
penters, and other tradesmen; others were employed
to make mortar. The next year they were taught
to drive the mules, the third to make *adobe* for
building; the fourth year they learned to ride horses
bareback, the fifth they were taught to ride in the
saddle while using firearms. At the age of six-
teen these boys became soldiers. They were then
married to the young negresses who had meanwhile
been taught cooking and washing in the Sultan's
palaces—except those who were pretty, and these

were given a musical education, after which each one received a wedding-dress and a marriage settlement, and was handed over to her husband.

"All the children of these couples were in due time destined for the Black Army, or for domestic service in the palaces. Every year the Sultan went to the camp at Mechra Erremel and brought back the children. The Black Army numbered one hundred and fifty thousand men, of whom part were at Erremel, part at Meknez, and the rest in the seventy-six forts which the Sultan built for them throughout his domain. May the Lord be merciful to his memory!"

Such was the army by means of which Ismaël enforced the *corvée* on his undisciplined tribes. Many thousands of lives went to the building of imperial Meknez; but his subjects would scarcely have sufficed if he had not been able to add to them twenty-five thousand Christian captives.

M. Augustin Bernard, in his admirable book on Morocco, says that the seventeenth century was "the golden age of piracy" in Morocco; and the great Ismaël was no doubt one of its chief promoters. One understands his unwillingness to come to an agreement with his great friend and competitor, Louis XIV, on the difficult subject of the ransom of Christian captives when one reads in the admiring Ezziani that it took fifty-five thousand prisoners and captives to execute his architectural conceptions.

"These prisoners, by day, were occupied on various tasks; at night they were locked into subterranean dungeons. Any prisoner who died at his task was *built into the wall he was building.*" (This statement is confirmed by John Windus, the English traveller who visited the court of Moulay-Ismaël in the Sultan's old age.) Many Europeans must have succumbed quickly to the heat and the lash, for the wall-builders were obliged to make each stroke in time with their neighbors, and were bastinadoed mercilessly if they broke the rhythm; and there is little doubt that the expert artisans of France, Italy and Spain were even dearer to the old architectural madman than the friendship of the palace-building despot across the sea.

Ezziani's chronicle dates from the first part of the nineteenth century, and is an Arab's colorless panegyric of a great Arab ruler; but John Windus,

the Englishman who accompanied Commodore
Stewart's embassy to Meknez in 1721, saw the imperial palaces and their builder with his own eyes,
and described them with the vivacity of a foreigner struck by every contrast.

Moulay-Ismaël was then about eighty-seven
years old, "a middle-sized man, who has the remains of a good face, with nothing of a negro's
features, though his mother was a black. He has
a high nose, which is pretty long from the eyebrows
downward, and thin. He has lost all his teeth, and
breathes short, as if his lungs were bad, coughs and
spits pretty often, which never falls to the ground,
men being always ready with handkerchiefs to receive it. His beard is thin and very white, his eyes
seem to have been sparkling, but their vigor de-
cayed through age, and his cheeks very much sunk
in."

Such was the appearance of this extraordinary
man, who deceived, tortured, betrayed, assassinated, terrorized and mocked his slaves, his subjects,
his women and children and his ministers like any
other half-savage Arab despot, but who yet managed through his long reign to maintain a barbar-

ous empire, to police the wilderness, and give at least an appearance of prosperity and security where all had before been chaos.

The English emissaries appear to have been much struck by the magnificence of his palaces, then in all the splendor of novelty, and gleaming with marbles brought from Volubilis and Salé. Windus extols in particular the sunken gardens of cypress, pomegranate and orange trees, some of them laid out seventy feet below the level of the palace-courts; the exquisite plaster fretwork; the miles of tessellated walls and pavement made in the finely patterned mosaic work of Fez; and the long terrace walk trellised with "vines and other greens" leading from the palace to the famous stables, and over which it was the Sultan's custom to drive in a chariot drawn by women and eunuchs.

Moulay-Ismaël received the English ambassador with every show of pomp and friendship, and immediately "made him a present" of a handful of young English captives; but just as the negotiations were about to be concluded Commodore Stewart was privately advised that the Sultan had no intention of allowing the rest of the English to be ransomed. Luckily a diplomatically composed letter, addressed by the English envoy to one of the favorite wives, resulted in Ismaël's changing his mind, and the captives were finally given up, and departed with their rescuers. As one stands in the fiery sun, among the monstrous ruins of those tragic walls, one pictures the other Christian captives pausing for a second, at the risk of death, in the rhythmic beat of their labor, to watch the little train of their companions winding away across the desert to freedom.

On the way back through the long streets that lead to the ruins we noticed, lying by the roadside, the shafts of fluted columns, blocks of marble, Roman capitals: fragments of the long loot of Salé and Volubilis. We asked how they came there, and were told that, according to a tradition still believed in the country, when the prisoners and captives who were dragging the building materials toward the palace under the blistering sun heard of the old Sultan's death, they dropped their loads with one accord and fled. At the same moment every worker on the walls flung down his trowel or hod, every slave of the palaces stopped grinding or scouring or drawing water or carrying faggots or polishing the miles of tessellated floors; so that, when the tyrant's heart stopped beating, at that very instant life ceased to circulate in the huge house he had built, and in all its members it became a carcass for his carcass.

III

FEZ

III

FEZ

I

THE FIRST VISION

MANY-WALLED Fez rose up before us out of the plain toward the end of the day. The walls and towers we saw were those of the upper town, Fez Eldjid (the New), which lies on the edge of the plateau and hides from view Old Fez tumbling down below it into the ravine of the Oued Fez. Thus approached, the city presents to view only a long line of ramparts and fortresses, merging into the wide, tawny plain and framed in barren mountains. Not a house is visible outside the walls, except, at a respectful distance, the few unobtrusive buildings of the European colony; and not a village breaks the desolation of the landscape.

As we drew nearer, the walls towered close over us, and skirting them we came to a bare space out-

side a great horseshoe gate, and found ourselves
suddenly in the foreground of a picture by Carpaccio or Bellini.   Where else had one seen just those
rows of white-turbaned majestic figures, squatting
in the dust under lofty walls, all the pale faces
ringed in curling beards turned to the story-teller
in the centre of the group?   Transform the story-
teller into a rapt young Venetian, and you have
the audience and the foreground of Carpaccio's
"Preaching of St. Stephen," even to the camels
craning inquisitive necks above the turbans.   Every
step of the way in North Africa corroborates the
close observation of the early travellers, whether
painters or narrators, and shows the unchanged
character of the Oriental life that the Venetians
pictured, and Leo Africanus and Windus and
Charles Cochelet described.

There was time, before sunset, to go up to the
hill, from which the ruined tombs of the Merinid
Sultans look down over the city they made glorious.
After the savage massacre of foreign residents in
1912 the French encircled the heights commanding
Fez with one of their admirably engineered military
roads, and in a few minutes our motor had climbed

to the point from which the great dynasty of artist-Sultans dreamed of looking down forever on their capital.

Nothing endures in Islam, except what human inertia has left standing and its own solidity has preserved from the elements. Or rather, nothing remains intact, and nothing wholly perishes, but the architecture, like all else, lingers on half-ruined and half-unchanged. The Merinid tombs, however, are only hollow shells and broken walls, grown part of the brown cliff they cling to. No one thinks of them save as an added touch of picturesqueness where all is picturesque: they survive as the best point from which to look down at Fez.

There it lies, outspread in golden light, roofs, terraces, and towers sliding over the plain's edge in a rush dammed here and there by barriers of cypress and ilex, but growing more precipitous as the ravine of the Fez narrows downward with the fall of the river. It is as though some powerful enchanter, after decreeing that the city should be hurled into the depths, had been moved by its beauty, and with a wave of his wand held it suspended above destruction.

FEZ

At first the eye takes in only this impression of a
great city over a green abyss; then the complex
scene begins to define itself. All around are the
outer lines of ramparts, walls beyond walls, their
crenellations climbing the heights, their angle fortresses dominating the precipices. Almost on a
level with us lies the upper city, the aristocratic
Fez Eldjid of painted palaces and gardens; then, as
the houses close in and descend more abruptly,
terraces, minarets, domes, and long reed-thatched
roofs of the bazaars, all gather around the green-
tiled tomb of Moulay Idriss, and the tower of the
Almohad mosque of El Kairouiyin, which adjoin
each other in the depths of Fez, and form its central sanctuary.

From the Merinid hill we had noticed a long
façade among the cypresses and fruit-trees of Eldjid. This was Bou-Jeloud, the old summer-palace
of the Sultan's harem, now the house of the Resident-General, where lodgings had been prepared
for us.

The road descended again, crossing the Oued Fez
by one of the fine old single-arch bridges that mark

the architectural link between Morocco and Spain.
We skirted high walls, wayside pools, and dripping
mill-wheels; then one of the city gates engulfed us,
and we were in the waste spaces of intramural Fez,
formerly the lines of defense of a rich and perpetually menaced city, now chiefly used for refuse-
heaps, open-air fondaks, and dreaming-places for
rows of Lazaruses rolled in their cerements in the
dust.

Through another gate and more walls we came
to an arch in the inner line of defense. Beyond
that, the motor paused before a green door, where
a Cadi in a silken caftan received us. Across
squares of orange-trees divided by running water
we were led to an arcaded apartment hung with
Moroccan embroideries and lined with wide divans;
the hall of reception of the Resident-General.
Through its arches were other tiled distances, fountains, arcades; beyond, in greener depths, the
bright blossoms of a flower-garden. Such was our
first sight of Bou-Jeloud, once the summer-palace
of the wives of Moulay Hafid.

Upstairs, from a room walled and ceiled with
cedar, and decorated with the bold rose-pink em-

broideries of Salé and the intricate old needlework
of Fez, I looked out over the upper city toward the
mauve and tawny mountains.

Just below the window the flat roofs of a group
of little houses descended like the steps of an irregu-
lar staircase. Between them rose a few cypresses
and a green minaret; out of the court of one house
an ancient fig-tree thrust its twisted arms. The
sun had set, and one after another bright figures
appeared on the roofs. The children came first,
hung with silver amulets and amber beads, and
pursued by negresses in striped turbans, who bus-
tled up with rugs and matting; then the mothers
followed more indolently, released from their ashy
mufflings and showing, under their light veils, long
earrings from the *Mellah** and caftans of pale green
or peach color.

The houses were humble ones, such as grow up
in the cracks of a wealthy quarter, and their inhabitants doubtless small folk; but in the enchanted
African twilight the terraces blossomed like gardens, and when the moon rose and the muezzin
called from the minaret, the domestic squabbles

* The Ghetto in African towns. All the jewellers in Morocco are Jews.

and the shrill cries from roof to roof became part of a story in Bagdad, overheard a thousand years ago by that arch-detective Haroun-al-Raschid.

II

FEZ ELDJID

It is usual to speak of Fez as very old, and the term seems justified when one remembers that the palace of Bou-Jeloud stands on the site of an Almoravid Kasbah of the eleventh century, that when that Kasbah was erected Fez Elbali had already existed for three hundred years, that El Kairouiyin is the contemporary of Sant' Ambrogio of Milan, and that the original mosque of Moulay Idriss II was built over his grave in the eighth century.

Fez is, in fact, the oldest city in Morocco without a Phenician or a Roman past, and has preserved more traces than any other of its architectural flowering-time; yet it would be truer to say of it, as of all Moroccan cities, that it has no age, since its seemingly immutable shape is forever crumbling and being renewed on the old lines.

When we rode forth the next day to visit some

of the palaces of Eldjid our pink-saddled mules carried us at once out of the bounds of time. How
associate anything so precise and Occidental as
years or centuries with these visions of frail splendor seen through cypresses and roses? The Cadis
in their multiple muslins, who received us in secret doorways and led us by many passages into
the sudden wonder of gardens and fountains;
the bright-earringed negresses peering down from
painted balconies; the pilgrims and clients dozing
in the sun against hot walls; the deserted halls with
plaster lace-work and gold pendentives in tiled
niches; the Venetian chandeliers and tawdry rococo
beds, the terraces from which pigeons whirled up in
a white cloud while we walked on a carpet of their
feathers—were all these the ghosts of vanished
state, or the actual setting of the life of some rich
merchant with "business connections" in Liverpool
and Lyons, or some government official at that
very moment speeding to Meknez or Casablanca
in his sixty h. p. motor?

We visited old palaces and new, inhabited and
abandoned, and over all lay the same fine dust of
oblivion, like the silvery mould on an overripe

From a photograph from the Service des Beaux-Arts au Maroc

Fez Eldjid (the upper city)

fruit. Overripeness is indeed the characteristic of this rich and stagnant civilization. Buildings, people, customs, seem all about to crumble and fall of their own weight: the present is a perpetually prolonged past. To touch the past with one's hands is realized only in dreams; and in Morocco the dream-feeling envelopes one at every step. One trembles continually lest the "Person from Porlock" should step in.

He is undoubtedly on the way; but Fez had not heard of him when we rode out that morning. Fez Eldjid, the "New Fez" of palaces and government buildings, was founded in the fourteenth century by the Merinid princes, and probably looks much as it did then. The palaces in their overgrown gardens, with pale-green trellises dividing the rose-beds from the blue-and-white tiled paths, and fountains in fluted basins of Italian marble, all had the same drowsy charm; yet the oldest were built not more than a century or two ago, others within the last fifty years; and at Marrakech, later in our journey, we were to visit a sumptuous dwelling where plaster-cutters and ceramists from Fez were actually repeating with wonderful skill and spon-

taneity, the old ornamentation of which the threads
run back to Rome and Damascus.

Of really old private dwellings, palaces or rich
men's houses, there are surprisingly few in Morocco.
It is hard to guess the age of some of the featureless
houses propping each other's flanks in old Fez or
old Salé; but people rich enough to rebuild have
always done so, and the passion for building seems
allied, in this country of inconsequences, to the
supine indifference that lets existing constructions
crumble back to clay. "Dust to dust" should have
been the motto of the Moroccan palace-builders.

Fez possesses one old secular building, a fine fondak of the fifteenth century; but in Morocco, as a
rule, only mosques and the tombs of saints are preserved—none too carefully—and even the strong
stone buildings of the Almohads have been allowed
to fall to ruin, as at Chella and Rabat. This indifference to the completed object—which is like a
kind of collective exaggeration of the artist's indifference to his completed work—has resulted in the
total disappearance of the furniture and works of
art which must have filled the beautiful buildings
of the Merinid period. Neither pottery nor brass-

work nor enamels nor fine hangings survive; there is no parallel in Morocco to the textiles of Syria, the potteries of Persia, the Byzantine ivories or enamels. It has been said that the Moroccan is always a nomad, who lives in his house as if it were a tent; but this is not a conclusive answer to any one who knows the passion of the modern Moroccan for European furniture. When one reads the list of the treasures contained in the palaces of the mediæval Sultans of Egypt one feels sure that, if artists were lacking in Morocco, the princes and merchants who brought skilled craftsmen across the desert to build their cities must also have imported treasures to adorn them. Yet, as far as is known, the famous fourteenth-century bronze chandelier of Tetuan, and the fine old ritual furniture reported to be contained in certain mosques, are the only important works of art in Morocco later in date than the Roman *sloughi* of Volubilis.

III

FEZ ELBALI

THE distances in Fez are so great and the streets so narrow, and in some quarters so crowded, that all but saints or humble folk go about on mule-back.

In the afternoon, accordingly, the pink mules came again, and we set out for the long tunnel-like street that leads down the hill to the Fez Elbali.

"Look out—'ware heads!" our leader would call back at every turn, as our way shrank to a black passage under a house bestriding the street, or a caravan of donkeys laden with obstructive reeds or branches of dates made the passers-by flatten themselves against the walls.

On each side of the street the houses hung over us like fortresses, leaning across the narrow strip of blue and throwing out great beams and buttresses to prop each other's bulging sides. Windows there were none on the lower floors; only here and there an iron-barred slit stuffed with rags and immemorial filth, from which a lean cat would suddenly spring out, and scuttle off under an archway like a witch's familiar.

Fez—a red-roofed street

Some of these descending lanes were packed with people, others as deserted as a cemetery; and it was strange to pass from the thronged streets leading to the bazaars to the profound and secretive silence of a quarter of well-to-do dwelling-houses, where only a few veiled women attended by negro slaves moved noiselessly over the clean cobblestones, and the sound of fountains and runnels came from hidden courtyards and over garden-walls.

This noise of water is as characteristic of Fez as of Damascus. The Oued Fez rushes through the heart of the town, bridged, canalized, built over, and ever and again bursting out into tumultuous falls and pools shadowed with foliage. The central artery of the city is not a street but a waterfall; and tales are told of the dark uses to which, even now, the underground currents are put by some of the dwellers behind the blank walls and scented gardens of those highly respectable streets.

The crowd in Oriental cities is made up of many elements, and in Morocco Turks, Jews and infidels, Berbers of the mountains, fanatics of the confraternities, Soudanese blacks and haggard Blue Men of the Souss, jostle the merchants and government

officials with that democratic familiarity which goes
side by side with abject servility in this land of perpetual contradictions. But Fez is above all the
city of wealth and learning, of universities and
counting-houses, and the merchant and the *oulama**
—the sedentary and luxurious types—prevail.

The slippered Fazi merchant, wrapped in white
muslins and securely mounted on a broad velvet
saddle-cloth anchored to the back of a broad mule,
is as unlike the Arab horseman of the desert as Mr.
Tracy Tupman was unlike the Musketeers of
Dumas. Ease, music, money-making, the affairs
of his harem and the bringing-up of his children,
are his chief interests, and his plump pale face with
long-lashed hazel eyes, his curling beard and fat
womanish hands, recall the portly potentates of
Hindu miniatures, dreaming among houris beside
lotus-tanks.

These personages, when they ride abroad, are
preceded by a swarthy footman, who keeps his hand
on the embroidered bridle; and the government
officers and dignitaries of the *Makhzen*† are usually
escorted by several mounted officers of their house-

* Learned man, doctor of the university.　　† The Sultan's government.

[90]

hold, with a servant to each mule. The cry of the
runners scatters the crowd, and even the panniered
donkeys and perpetually astonished camels some-
how contrive to become two-dimensional while the
white procession goes by.

Then the populace closes in again, so quickly
and densely that it seems impossible it could ever
have been parted, and negro water-carriers, muffled
women, beggars streaming with sores, sinewy and
greasy "saints," Soudanese sorcerers hung with
amulets made of sardine-boxes and hares'-feet, long-
lashed boys of the Chleuh in clean embroidered caftans, Jews in black robes and skull-caps, university
students carrying their prayer-carpets, bangled and
spangled black women, scrofulous children with
gazelle eyes and mangy skulls, and blind men tap-
ping along with linked arms and howling out verses
of the Koran, surge together in a mass drawn by
irresistible suction to the point where the bazaars
converge about the mosques of Moulay Idriss and
El Kairouiyin.

Seen from a terrace of the upper town, the long
thatched roofing of El Attarine, the central bazaar
of Fez, promises fantastic revelations of native life;

but the dun-colored crowds moving through its checkered twilight, the lack of carved shop-fronts and gaily adorned coffee-houses, and the absence of the painted coffers and vivid embroideries of Tunis, remind one that Morocco is a melancholy country, and Fez a profoundly melancholy city.

Dust and ashes, dust and ashes, echoes from the gray walls, the mouldering thatch of the *souks*, the long lamentable song of the blind beggars sitting in rows under the feet of the camels and asses. No young men stroll through the bazaar in bright caftans, with roses and jasmine behind their ears, no pedlars offer lemonade and sweetmeats and golden fritters, no flower-sellers pursue one with tight bunches of orange-blossom and little pink roses. The well-to-do ride by in white, and the rest of the population goes mournfully in earth-color.

But gradually one falls under the spell of another influence—the influence of the Atlas and the desert. Unknown Africa seems much nearer to Morocco than to the white towns of Tunis and the smiling oases of South Algeria. One feels the nearness of Marrakech at Fez, and at Marrakech that of Timbuctoo.

FEZ

Fez is sombre, and the bazaars clustered about its holiest sanctuaries form its most sombre quarter. Dusk falls there early, and oil-lanterns twinkle in the merchants' niches while the clear African daylight still lies on the gardens of upper Fez. This twilight adds to the mystery of the *souks*, making them, in spite of profane noise and crowding and filth, an impressive approach to the sacred places.

Until a year or two ago, the precincts around Moulay Idriss and El Kairouiyin were *horm*, that is, cut off from the unbeliever. Heavy beams of wood barred the end of each *souk*, shutting off the sanctuaries, and the Christian could only conjecture what lay beyond. Now he knows in part; for, though the beams have not been lowered, all comers may pass under them to the lanes about the mosques, and even pause a moment in their open doorways. Farther one may not go, for the shrines of Morocco are still closed to unbelievers; but whoever knows Cordova, or has stood under the arches of the Great Mosque of Kairouan, can reconstruct something of the hidden beauties of its namesake, the "Mosque Kairouan" of western Africa.

Once under the bars, the richness of the old

Moorish Fez presses upon one with unexpected beauty. Here is the graceful tiled fountain of Nedjarine, glittering with the unapproachable blues and greens of ceramic mosaics; near it, the court-yard of the Fondak Nedjarine, oldest and stateliest of Moroccan inns, with triple galleries of sculptured cedar rising above arcades of stone. A little farther on lights and incense draw one to a threshold where it is well not to linger unduly. Under a deep arch-way, between booths where gay votive candles are sold, the glimmer of hanging lamps falls on patches of gilding and mosaic, and on veiled women pros-trating themselves before an invisible shrine—for this is the vestibule of the mosque of Moulay Idriss, where, on certain days of the week, women are admitted to pray.

Moulay Idriss was not built over the grave of the Fatimite prophet, first of the name, whose bones lie in the Zerhoun above his sacred town. The mosque of Fez grew up around the tomb of his posthumous son, Moulay Idriss II, who, descend-ing from the hills, fell upon a camp of Berbers on an affluent of the Sebou, and there laid the founda-tions of Fez, and of the Moroccan Empire.

Fez—the Nedjarine fountain

FEZ

Of the original monument it is said that little
remains. The *zaouïa** which encloses it dates
from the reign of Moulay-Ismaël, the seventeenth-
century Sultan of Meknez, and the mosque itself,
and the green minaret shooting up from the very
centre of old Fez, were not built until 1820. But a
rich surface of age has already formed on all these
disparate buildings, and the over-gorgeous details
of the shrines and fountains set in their outer walls
are blended into harmony by a film of incense-
smoke, and the grease of countless venerating lips
and hands.

Featureless walls of mean houses close in again
at the next turn; but a few steps farther another
archway reveals another secret scene. This time it
is a corner of the jealously guarded court of ablutions in the great mosque El Kairouiyin, with the
twin green-roofed pavilions that are so like those of
the Alhambra.

Those who have walked around the outer walls
of the mosque of the other Kairouan, and recall the
successive doors opening into the forecourt and
into the mosque itself, will be able to guess at the

* Moslem monastery.

plan of the church of Fez. The great Almohad
sanctuary of Tunisia is singularly free from para-
sitic buildings, and may be approached as easily as
that of Cordova; but the approaches of El Kairouiyin are so built up that one never knows at which
turn of the labyrinth one may catch sight of its
court of fountains, or peep down the endless colonnades of which the Arabs say: "The man who
should try to count the columns of Kairouiyin
would go mad."

Marble floors, heavy whitewashed piers, pros-
trate figures in the penumbra, rows of yellow slippers outside in the sunlight—out of such glimpses
one must reconstruct a vision of the long vistas of
arches, the blues and golds of the *mirhab*,* the
lustre of bronze chandeliers, and the ivory inlaying
of the twelfth-century *minbar*† of ebony and san-
dalwood.

No Christian footstep has yet profaned Kairouiyin, but fairly definite information as to its plan
has been gleaned by students of Moroccan art.
The number of its "countless" columns has been
counted, and it is known that, to the right of the

* Niche in the sanctuary of mosques   † Movable pulpit.

mirhab, carved cedar doors open into a mortuary chapel called "the mosque of the dead"—and also that in this chapel, on Fridays, old books and precious manuscripts are sold by auction.

This odd association of uses recalls the fact that Kairouiyin is not only a church but a library, the University of Fez as well as its cathedral. The beautiful Medersas with which the Merinids adorned the city are simply the lodging-houses of the students; the classes are all held in the courts and galleries adjoining the mosque.

El Kairouiyin was originally an oratory built in the ninth century by Fatmah, whose father had migrated from Kairouan to Fez. Later it was enlarged, and its cupola was surmounted by the talismans which protect sacred edifices against rats, scorpions and serpents; but in spite of these precautions all animal life was not successfully exorcised from it. In the twelfth century, when the great gate Ech Chemmâïn was building, a well was discovered under its foundations. The mouth of the well was obstructed by an immense tortoise; but when the workmen attempted to take the tortoise out she said: "Burn me rather than take me away from here." They respected her wishes and built her into the foundations; and since then women who suffer from the back-ache have only to come and sit on the bench above the well to be cured.

The actual mosque, or "praying-hall," is said to be formed of a rectangle or double cube of 90 metres by 45, and this vast space is equally divided by rows of horseshoe arches resting on whitewashed piers on which the lower part is swathed in finely patterned matting from Salé. Fifteen monumental doorways lead into the mosque. Their doors are of cedar, heavily barred and ornamented with wrought iron, and one of them bears the name of the artisan, and the date 531 of the Hegira (the first half of the twelfth century). The mosque also contains the two halls of audience of the Cadi, of which one has a graceful exterior façade with coupled lights under horseshoe arches; the library, whose 20,000 volumes are reported to have dwindled to about a thousand; the chapel where the Masters of the Koran recite the sacred text in fulfilment of pious bequests; the "museum" in the upper part of the minaret, wherein a remarkable collection of ancient astronomical instruments is said to be preserved; and the *mestonda*, or raised hall above the court, where women come to pray.

But the crown of El Kairouiyin is the Merinid court of ablutions. This inaccessible wonder lies close under the Medersa Attarine, one of the oldest and most beautiful collegiate buildings of Fez; and through the kindness of the Director of Fine Arts, who was with us, we were taken up to the roof of the Medersa and allowed to look down into the enclosure.

It is so closely guarded from below that from our secret coign of vantage we seemed to be looking down into the heart of forbidden things. Spacious and serene the great tiled cloister lay beneath us, water spilling over from a central basin of marble with a cool sound to which lesser fountains made answer from under the pyramidal green roofs of the twin pavilions. It was near the prayer-hour, and worshippers were flocking in, laying off their shoes and burnouses, washing their faces at the fountains and their feet in the central tank, or stretching themselves out in the shadow of the enclosing arcade.

This, then, was the famous court "so cool in the

great heats that seated by thy beautiful jet of water
I feel the perfection of bliss"—as the learned doctor Abou Abd Allah el Maghili sang of it; the court
in which the students gather from the adjoining
halls after having committed to memory the principles of grammar in prose and verse, the "science
of the reading of the Koran," the invention, exposition and ornaments of style, law, medicine, theology, metaphysics and astronomy, as well as the
talismanic numbers, and the art of ascertaining by
calculation the influences of the angels, the spirits
and the heavenly bodies, "the names of the victor
and the vanquished, and of the desired object and
the person who desires it."

Such is the twentieth-century curriculum of the
University of Fez. Repetition is the rule of Arab
education as it is of Arab ornament. The teaching
of the University is based entirely on the mediæval
principle of mnemonics; and as there are no exami-
nations, no degrees, no limits to the duration of any
given course, nor is any disgrace attached to slow-
ness in learning, it is not surprising that many students, coming as youths, linger by the fountain of
Kairouiyin till their hair is gray. One well-known

oulama has lately finished his studies after twenty-seven years at the University, and is justly proud of the length of his stay. The life of the scholar is easy, the way of knowledge is long, the contrast exquisite between the foul lanes and noisy bazaars outside and this cool heaven of learning. No wonder the students of Kairouiyin say with the tortoise: "Burn me rather than take me away."

IV

EL ANDALOUS AND THE POTTERS' FIELD

OUTSIDE the sacred precincts of Moulay Idriss and Kairouiyin, on the other side of the Oued Fez, lies El Andalous, the mosque which the Andalusian Moors built when they settled in Fez in the ninth century.

It stands apart from the bazaars, on higher ground, and though it is not *horm* we found it less easy to see than the more famous mosques, since the Christian loiterer in its doorways is more quickly noticed. The Fazi are not yet used to seeing unbelievers near their sacred places. It is only in the tumult and confusion of the *souks* that one can linger on the edge of the inner mysteries without becoming aware of attracting sullen looks; and my only impression of El Andalous is of a magnificent Almohad door and the rich blur of an interior in which there was no time to single out the details.

Turning from its forbidden and forbidding threshold we rode on through a poor quarter which leads to the great gate of Bab F'touh. Beyond the gate rises a dusty rocky slope extending to the outer walls—one of those grim intramural deserts that girdle Fez with desolation. This one is strewn with gravestones, not enclosed, but, as in most Moroccan cemeteries, simply cropping up like nettles between the rocks and out of the flaming dust. Here and there among the slabs rises a well-curb or a crumbling *koubba*. A solitary palm shoots up beside one of the shrines. And between the crowded graves the caravan trail crosses from the outer to the inner gate, and perpetual lines of camels and donkeys trample the dead a little deeper into the dusty earth.

This Bab F'touh cemetery is also a kind of fondak. Poor caravans camp there under the walls in a mire of offal and chicken-feathers and stripped date-branches prowled through by wolfish dogs and buzzed over by fat blue flies. Camel-drivers squat beside iron kettles over heaps of embers, sorcerers from the Sahara offer their amulets to negro women, peddlers with portable wooden booths sell greasy cakes that look as if they had been made out of the garbage of the caravans, and in and out among the unknown dead and sleeping saints circulates the squalid indifferent life of the living poor.

A walled lane leads down from Bab F'touh to a lower slope, where the Fazi potters have their baking-kilns. Under a series of grassy terraces overgrown with olives we saw the archaic ovens and dripping wheels which produce the earthenware sold in the *souks*. It is a primitive and homely ware, still fine in shape, though dull in color and monotonous in pattern; and stacked on the red earth under the olives, the rows of jars and cups, in their unglazed and unpainted state, showed their classical descent more plainly than after they have been decorated.

This green quiet hollow, where turbaned figures were moving attentively among the primitive ovens, so near to the region of flies and offal we had just left, woke an old phrase in our memories, and as our mules stumbled back over the graves of Bab F'touh we understood the grim meaning of the words: "They carried him out and buried him in the Potters' Field."

V

MEDERSAS, BAZAARS AND AN OASIS

FEZ, for two centuries and more, was in a double sense the capital of Morocco:'the centre of its trade as well as of its culture.

Culture, in fact, came to northwest Africa chiefly through the Merinid princes. The Almohads had erected great monuments from Rabat to Marrakech, and had fortified Fez; but their "mighty wasteful empire" fell apart like those that had preceded it. Stability had to come from the west; it was not till the Arabs had learned it through the Moors that Morocco produced a dynasty strong and enlightened enough to carry out the dream of its founders.

Whichever way the discussion sways as to the priority of eastern or western influences on Moroccan art—whether it came to her from Syria, and was thence passed on to Spain, or was first formed in Spain, and afterward modified by the Moroccan imagination—there can at least be no doubt that Fazi art and culture, in their prime, are partly the reflection of European civilization.

Fugitives from Spain came to the new city when Moulay Idriss founded it. One part of the town was given to them, and the river divided the Elbali of the Almohads into the two quarters of Kairouiyin and Andalous, which still retain their old names. But the full intellectual and artistic flowering of Fez was delayed till the thirteenth and fourteenth centuries. It seems as though the seeds of the new springtime of art, blown across the sea from re-awakening Europe, had at last given the weltering tribes of the desert the force to create their own type of beauty.

Nine Medersas sprang up in Fez, six of them built by the princes who were also creating the exquisite collegiate buildings of Salé, Rabat and old Meknez, and the enchanting mosque and minaret of Chella. The power of these rulers also was in perpetual flux; they were always at war with the Sultans of Tlemcen, the Christians of Spain, the

princes of northern Algeria and Tunis. But during
the fourteenth century they established a rule wide
and firm enough to permit of the great outburst of
art and learning which produced the Medersas of
Fez.

Until a year or two ago these collegiate buildings
were as inaccessible as the mosques; but now that
the French government has undertaken their resto-
ration strangers may visit them under the guidance
of the Fine Arts Department.

All are built on the same plan, the plan of Salé
and Rabat, which (as M. Tranchant de Lunel*
has pointed out) became, with slight modifications,
that of the rich private houses of Morocco. But
interesting as they are in plan and the application
of ornament, their main beauty lies in their details:
in the union of chiselled plaster with the delicate
mosaic work of niches and revêtements; the web-like
arabesques of the upper walls and the bold, almost
Gothic sculpture of the cedar architraves and corbels supporting them. And when all these details
are enumerated, and also the fretted panels of
cedar, the bronze doors with their great shield-like

* In *France-Maroc, No.* 1.

bosses, and the honeycombings and rufflings of the gilded ceilings, there still remains the general tinge of dry disintegration, as though all were perishing of a desert fever—that, and the final wonder of seeing before one, in such a setting, the continuance of the very life that went on there when the tiles were set and the gold was new on the ceilings.

For these tottering Medersas, already in the hands of the restorers, are still inhabited. As long as the stairway holds and the balcony has not rotted from its corbels, the students of the University see no reason for abandoning their lodgings above the cool fountain and the house of prayer. The strange men giving incomprehensible orders for unnecessary repairs need not disturb their meditations; and when the hammering grows too loud the *oulamas* have only to pass through the silk market or the *souk* of the embroiderers to the mosque of Kairouiyin, and go on weaving the pattern of their dreams by the fountain of perfect bliss.

One reads of the bazaars of Fez that they have been for centuries the central market of the country. Here are to be found not only the silks and pottery, the Jewish goldsmiths' work, the arms and embroidered saddlery which the city itself produces, but "morocco" from Marrakech, rugs, tent-hangings and matting from Rabat and Salé, grain baskets from Moulay Idriss, daggers from the Souss, and whatever European wares the native markets consume. One looks, on the plan of Fez, at the space covered by the bazaars; one breasts the swarms that pour through them from dawn to dusk—and one remains perplexed, disappointed. They are less "Oriental" than one had expected, if "Oriental" means color and gaiety.

Sometimes, on occasion, it does mean that: as, for instance, when a procession passes bearing the gifts for a Jewish wedding. The gray crowd makes way for a group of musicians in brilliant caftans, and following them comes a long file of women with uncovered faces and bejewelled necks, balancing on their heads the dishes the guests have sent to the feast—*kouskous*, sweet creams and syrups, "gazelles' horns" of sugar and almonds—in delicately woven baskets, each covered with several squares of bright gauze edged with gold. Then one remembers the marketing of the Lady of "The Three Calendars,"

From a photograph from the Service des Beaux-Arts au Maroc

Fez—the bazaars. A view of the Souk el Attarine and the Quaisarya (silk market)

and Fez again becomes the Bagdad of Al Raschid.

But when no exceptional events, processions, ceremonies and the like brighten the underworld of the *souks*, their look is uniformly melancholy. The gay bazaars, the gaily-painted houses, the flowers and flute-playing of North Africa, are found in her Mediterranean ports, in contact with European influences. The farther west she extends, the more she becomes self-contained, sombre, uninfluenced, a gloomy fanatic with her back to the walls of the Atlantic and the Atlas. Color and laughter lie mostly along the trade-routes, where the peoples of the world come and go in curiosity and rivalry. This ashen crowd swarming gloomily through the dark tunnels represents the real Moghreb that is close to the wild tribes of the "hinterland" and the grim feudal fortresses of the Atlas. How close, one has only to go out to Sefrou on a market-day to see.

Sefrou is a military outpost in an oasis under the Atlas, about forty miles south of Fez. To most people the word "oasis" evokes palms and sand; but though Morocco possesses many oases it has no pure sand and few palms. I remember it as a considerable event when I discovered one from my lofty window at Bou-Jeloud.

The *bled* is made of very different stuff from the sand-ocean of the Sahara. The light plays few tricks with it. Its monotony is wearisome rather than impressive, and the fact that it is seldom without some form of dwarfish vegetation makes the transition less startling when the alluvial green is finally reached. One had always half expected it, and it does not spring at a djinn's wave out of sterile gold.

But the fact brings its own compensations. Moroccan oases differ one from another far more than those of South Algeria and Tunisia. Some have no palms, others but a few, others are real palm-oases, though even in the south (at least on the hither side of the great Atlas) none spreads out a dense uniform roofing of metal-blue fronds like the date-oases of Biskra or Tozeur. As for Sefrou, which Foucauld called the most beautiful oasis of Morocco, it is simply an extremely fertile valley with vineyards and orchards stretching up to a fine background of mountains. But the fact that it lies just below the

Atlas makes it an important market-place and centre of caravans.

Though so near Fez it is still almost on the disputed border between the loyal and the "unsubmissive" tribes, those that are *Blad-Makhzen* (of the Sultan's government) and those that are against it. Until recently, therefore, it has been inaccessible to visitors, and even now a strongly fortified French post dominates the height above the town. Looking down from the fort, one distinguishes, through masses of many-tinted green, a suburb of Arab houses in gardens, and below, on the river, Sefrou itself, a stout little walled town with angle-towers defiantly thrust forth toward the Atlas. It is just outside these walls that the market is held.

It was swarming with hill-people the day we were there, and strange was the contrast between the crowd inside the circle of picketed horses and the white-robed cockneys from Rabat who fill the market-place of Salé. Here at last we were in touch with un-Arab Morocco, with Berbers of the *bled* and the hills, whose women know no veils and no seclusion, and who, under a thin surface of Mahometanism, preserve their old stone and animal worship, and all the gross fetichistic beliefs from which Mahomet dreamed of freeing Africa.

The men were lean and weather-bitten, some with negroid lips, others with beaked noses and gaunt cheek-bones, all muscular and fierce-looking. Some were wrapped in the black cloaks worn by the Blue Men of the Sahara,* with a great orange sun embroidered on the back; some tunicked like the Egyptian fellah, under a rough striped outer garment trimmed with bright tufts and tassels of wool. The men of the Rif had a braided lock on the shoulder, those of the Atlas a ringlet over each ear, and brown woollen scarfs wound round their temples, leaving the shaven crown bare.

The women, squatting among their kids and poultry and cheeses, glanced at us with brilliant hennaed eyes and smiles that lifted their short upper lips maliciously. Their thin faces were painted in stripes and patterns of indigo. Silver necklets covered their throats, long earrings dangled under the wool-embroidered kerchiefs bound about their temples with a twist of camel's hair, and below the cot-

* So called because of the indigo dye of their tunics, which leaves a permanent stain on their bodies

ton shifts fastened on their shoulders with silver
clasps their legs were bare to the knee, or covered
with leather leggings to protect them from the
thorny *bled*.

They seemed abler bargainers than the men, and
the play of expression on their dramatic and in-
tensely feminine faces as they wheedled the price
of a calf out of a fierce hillsman, or haggled over a
heap of dates that a Jew with greasy ringlets was
trying to secure for his secret distillery, showed that
they knew their superiority and enjoyed it.

Jews abounded in the market-place and also in
the town. Sefrou contains a large Israelite colony,
and after we had wandered through the steep
streets, over gushing waterfalls spanned by "ass-
backed" Spanish bridges, and through a thatched
souk smelling strong of camels and the desert, the
French commissioner (the only European in Sefrou)
suggested that it might interest us to visit the
Mellah.

It was our first sight of a typical Jewish quarter
in Africa. The *Mellah* of Fez was almost entirely
destroyed during the massacres of 1912 (which in-
cidentally included a *pogrom*), and its distinctive

character, happily for the inhabitants, has disappeared in the rebuilding. North African Jews are still compelled to live in ghettos, into which they are locked at night, as in France and Germany in the Middle Ages; and until lately the men have been compelled to go unarmed, to wear black gabardines and black slippers, to take off their shoes when they passed near a mosque or a saint's tomb, and in various other ways to manifest their subjection to the ruling race. Nowhere else do they live in conditions of such demoralizing promiscuity as in some of the cities of Morocco. They have so long been subject to unrestricted extortion on the part of the Moslems that even the wealthy Jews (who are numerous) have sunk to the habits and appearance of the poorest; and Sefrou, which has come so recently under French control, offers a good specimen of a *Mellah* before foreign sanitation has lighted up its dark places.

Dark indeed they were. After wandering through narrow and malodorous lanes, and slipping about in the offal of the *souks*, we were suddenly led under an arch over which should have been written "All light abandon—" and which made all we had seen before seem clean and bright and airy.

FEZ

The beneficent African sun dries up and purifies
the immemorial filth of Africa; where that sun
enters there is none of the foulness of damp. But
into the *Mellah* of Sefrou it never comes, for the
streets form a sort of subterranean rabbit-warren
under the upper stories of a solid agglomeration of
tall houses—a buried city lit even at midday by
oil-lamps hanging in the goldsmiths' shops and
under the archways of the black and reeking stair-
cases.

It was a Jewish feast-day. The Hebrew stalls in
the *souks* were closed, and the whole population of
the *Mellah* thronged its tunnels in holiday dress.
Hurrying past us were young women with plump
white faces and lovely eyes, turbaned in brilliant
gauzes, with draperies of dirty curtain muslin over
tawdry brocaded caftans. Their paler children
swarmed about them, little long-earringed girls like
wax dolls dressed in scraps of old finery, little boys
in tattered caftans with long-lashed eyes and wily
smiles; and, waddling in the rear, their unwieldy
grandmothers, huge lumps of tallowy flesh who
were probably still in the thirties.

With them were the men of the family, in black
gabardines and skull-caps: sallow striplings, incal-

culably aged ancestors, round-bellied husbands and fathers bumping along like black balloons; all hastening to the low doorways dressed with lamps and paper garlands behind which the feast was spread.

One is told that in cities like Fez and Marrakech the Hebrew quarter conceals flowery patios and gilded rooms with the heavy European furniture that rich Jews delight in. Perhaps even in the *Mellah* of Sefrou, among the ragged figures shuffling past us, there were some few with bags of gold in their walls and rich stuffs hid away in painted coffers; but for patios and flowers and daylight there seemed no room in the dark *bolgia* they inhabit. No wonder the babies of the Moroccan ghettos are nursed on date-brandy, and their elders doze away to death under its consoling spell.

VI

THE LAST GLIMPSE

It is well to bid good-by to Fez at night—a moonlight night for choice.

Then, after dining at the Arab inn of Fez Eldjid —where it might be inconvenient to lodge, but where it is extremely pleasant to eat *kouskous* under a grape-trellis in a tiled and fountained patio—this pleasure over, one may set out on foot and stray down the lanes toward Fez Elbali.

Not long ago the gates between the different quarters of the city used to be locked every night at nine o'clock, and the merchant who went out to dine in another part of the town had to lodge with his host. Now this custom has been given up, and one may roam about untroubled through the old quarters, grown as silent as the grave after the intense life of the bazaars has ceased at nightfall.

Nobody is in the streets: wandering from ghostly passage to passage, one hears no step but that of the watchman with staff and lantern. Presently there appears, far off, a light like a low-flying firefly; as it comes nearer, it is seen to proceed from the *Mellah* lamp of open-work brass that a servant carries ahead of two merchants on their way home from Elbali. The merchants are grave men: they move softly and slowly on their fat slippered feet, pausing from time to time in confidential talk. At last they stop before a house wall with a low blue door barred by heavy hasps of iron. The servant lifts the lamp and knocks. There is a long delay; then, with infinite caution, the door is opened a few inches, and another lifted light shines faintly on lustrous tiled walls, and on the face of a woman slave who quickly veils herself. Evidently the master is a man of standing, and the house well guarded. The two merchants touch each other on the right shoulder, one of them passes in, and his friend goes on through the moonlight, his servant's lantern dancing ahead.

But here we are in an open space looking down one of the descents to El Attarine. A misty radiance washes the tall houses, the garden-walls, the archways; even the moonlight does not whiten Fez, but only turns its gray to tarnished silver. Overhead in a tower window a single light twinkles: women's voices rise and fall on the roofs. In a rich man's doorway slaves are sleeping, huddled on the tiles. A cock crows from somebody's dunghill; a skeleton dog prowls by for garbage.

Everywhere is the loud rush or the low crooning of water, and over every wall comes the scent of jasmine and rose. Far off, from the red purgatory between the walls, sounds the savage thrum-thrum of a negro orgy; here all is peace and perfume. A minaret springs up between the roof like a palm, and from its balcony the little white figure bends over and drops a blessing on all the loveliness and all the squalor.

IV

MARRAKECH

IV

MARRAKECH

I

THE WAY THERE

THERE are countless Arab tales of evil Djinns who take the form of sandstorms and hot winds to overwhelm exhausted travellers.

In spite of the new French road between Rabat and Marrakech the memory of such tales rises up insistently from every mile of the level red earth and the desolate stony stretches of the *bled*. As long as the road runs in sight of the Atlantic breakers they give the scene freshness and life; but when it bends inland and stretches away across the wilderness the sense of the immensity and immobility of Africa descends on one with an intolerable oppression.

The road traverses no villages, and not even a ring of nomad tents is visible in the distance on the wide stretches of arable land. At infrequent intervals our motor passed a train of laden mules, or a group of peasants about a well, and sometimes, far off, a fortified farm profiled its thick-set angle-towers against the sky, or a white *koubba* floated like a mirage above the brush; but these rare signs of life intensified the solitude of the long miles between.

At midday we were refreshed by the sight of the little oasis around the military-post of Settat. We lunched there with the commanding officer, in a cool Arab house about a flowery patio; but that brief interval over, the fiery plain began again. After Settat the road runs on for miles across the waste to the gorge of the Oued Ouem; and beyond the river it climbs to another plain so desperate in its calcined aridity that the prickly scrub of the wilderness we had left seemed like the vegetation of an oasis. For fifty kilometres the earth under our wheels was made up of a kind of glistening red slag covered with pebbles and stones. Not the scantest and toughest of rock-growths thrust a leaf through its brassy surface; not a well-head or a darker depression of the rock gave sign of a trickle of water. Everything around us glittered with the same unmerciful dryness.

A long way ahead loomed the line of the Djebilets, the Djinn-haunted mountains guarding Marrakech on the north. When at last we reached them the wicked glister of their purple flanks seemed like a volcanic upheaval of the plain. For some time we had watched the clouds gathering over them, and as we got to the top of the defile rain was falling from a fringe of thunder to the south. Then the vapours lifted, and we saw below us another red plain with an island of palms in its centre. Mysteriously, from the heart of the palms, a tower shot up, as if alone in the wilderness; behind it stood the sun-streaked cliffs of the Atlas, with snow summits appearing and vanishing through the storm.

As we drove downward the rock gradually began to turn to red earth fissured by yellow streams, and stray knots of palms sprang up, lean and dishevelled, about well-heads where people were watering camels and donkeys. To the east, dominating the oasis, the twin peaked hills of the Ghilis, fortified to the crest, mounted guard over invisible Marrakech;

[125]

but still, above the palms, we saw only that lonely and triumphant tower.

Presently we crossed the Oued Tensif on an old bridge built by Moroccan engineers. Beyond the river were more palms, then olive-orchards, then the vague sketch of the new European settlement, with a few shops and cafés on avenues ending suddenly in clay pits, and at last Marrakech itself appeared to us, in the form of a red wall across a red wilderness.

We passed through a gate and were confronted by other ramparts. Then we entered an outskirt of dusty red lanes bordered by clay hovels with draped figures slinking by like ghosts. After that more walls, more gates, more endlessly winding lanes, more gates again, more turns, a dusty open space with donkeys and camels and negroes; a final wall with a great door under a lofty arch—and suddenly we were in the palace of the Bahia, among flowers and shadows and falling water.

MARRAKECH

II

THE BAHIA

WHOEVER would understand Marrakech must begin by mounting at sunset to the roof of the Bahia.

Outspread below lies the oasis-city of the south, flat and vast as the great nomad camp it really is, its low roofs extending on all sides to a belt of blue palms ringed with desert. Only two or three minarets and a few noblemen's houses among gardens break the general flatness; but they are hardly noticeable, so irresistibly is the eye drawn toward two dominant objects—the white wall of the Atlas and the red tower of the Koutoubya.

Foursquare, untapering, the great tower lifts its flanks of ruddy stone. Its large spaces of unornamented wall, its triple tier of clustered openings, lightening as they rise from the severe rectangular lights of the first stage to the graceful arcade below the parapet, have the stern harmony of the noblest architecture. The Koutoubya would be magnificent anywhere; in this flat desert it is grand enough to face the Atlas.

The Almohad conquerors who built the Kou-

toubya and embellished Marrakech dreamed a
dream of beauty that extended from the Guadal-
quivir to the Sahara; and at its two extremes they
placed their watch-towers. The Giralda watched
over civilized enemies in a land of ancient Roman
culture; the Koutoubya stood at the edge of the
world, facing the hordes of the desert.

The Almoravid princes who founded Marrakech
came from the black desert of Senegal; themselves
were leaders of wild hordes. In the history of
North Africa the same cycle has perpetually repeated itself. Generation after generation of chiefs
have flowed in from the desert or the mountains,
overthrown their predecessors, massacred, plun-
dered, grown rich, built sudden palaces, encouraged
their great servants to do the same; then fallen on
them, and taken their wealth and their palaces.
Usually some religious fury, some ascetic wrath
against the self-indulgence of the cities, has been
the motive of these attacks; but invariably the
same results followed, as they followed when the
Germanic barbarians descended on Italy. The conquerors, infected with luxury and mad with power,
built vaster palaces, planned grander cities; but

From a photograph from the Service des Beaux-Arts au Maroc

Marrakech—The "Little Garden" (with painted doors) in background,
Palace of the Bahia

Sultans and Viziers camped in their golden houses as if on the march, and the mud huts of the tribesmen within their walls were but one degree removed from the mud-walled tents of the *bled*.

This was more especially the case with Marrakech, a city of Berbers and blacks, and the last outpost against the fierce black world beyond the Atlas from which its founders came. When one looks at its site, and considers its history, one can only marvel at the height of civilization it attained.

The Bahia itself, now the palace of the Resident General, though built less than a hundred years ago, is typical of the architectural megalomania of the great southern chiefs. It was built by Ba-Ahmed, the all-powerful black Vizier of the Sultan Moulay-el-Hassan.* Ba-Ahmed was evidently an artist and an archæologist. His ambition was to re-create a Palace of Beauty such as the Moors had built in the prime of Arab art, and he brought to Marrakech skilled artificers of Fez, the last surviving masters of the mystery of chiselled plaster and ceramic mosaics and honeycombing of gilded cedar. They came, they built the Bahia, and it remains

* Moulay-el-Hassan reigned from 1873 to 1894

[129]

the loveliest and most fantastic of Moroccan palaces.

Court within court, garden beyond garden, reception halls, private apartments, slaves' quarters, sunny prophets' chambers on the roofs and baths in vaulted crypts, the labyrinth of passages and rooms stretches away over several acres of ground. A long court enclosed in pale-green trellis-work, where pigeons plume themselves about a great tank and the dripping tiles glitter with refracted sunlight, leads to the fresh gloom of a cypress garden, or under jasmine tunnels bordered with running water; and these again open on arcaded apartments faced with tiles and stucco-work, where, in a languid twilight, the hours drift by to the ceaseless music of the fountains.

The beauty of Moroccan palaces is made up of details of ornament and refinements of sensuous delight too numerous to record; but to get an idea of their general character it is worth while to cross the Court of Cypresses at the Bahia and follow a series of low-studded passages that turn on themselves till they reach the centre of the labyrinth. Here, passing by a low padlocked door leading to a

From a photograph by Félix, Marrakech   Marrakech—the great court, Palace of the Bahia

crypt, and known as the "Door of the Vizier's Treasure-House," one comes on a painted portal that opens into a still more secret sanctuary: The apartment of the Grand Vizier's Favourite.

This lovely prison, from which all sight and sound of the outer world are excluded, is built about an atrium paved with disks of turquoise and black and white. Water trickles from a central *vasca* of alabaster into a hexagonal mosaic channel in the pavement. The walls, which are at least twenty-five feet high, are roofed with painted beams resting on panels of traceried stucco in which is set a clerestory of jewelled glass. On each side of the atrium are long recessed rooms closed by vermilion doors painted with gold arabesques and vases of spring flowers; and into these shadowy inner rooms, spread with rugs and divans and soft pillows, no light comes except when their doors are opened into the atrium. In this fabulous place it was my good luck to be lodged while I was at Marrakech.

In a climate where, after the winter snow has melted from the Atlas, every breath of air for long months is a flame of fire, these enclosed rooms in the middle of the palaces are the only places of refuge from the heat. Even in October the temperature of the favourite's apartment was deliciously reviving after a morning in the bazaars or the dusty streets, and I never came back to its wet tiles and perpetual twilight without the sense of plunging into a deep sea-pool.

From far off, through circuitous corridors, came the scent of citron-blossom and jasmine, with sometimes a bird's song before dawn, sometimes a flute's wail at sunset, and always the call of the muezzin in the night; but no sunlight reached the apartment except in remote rays through the clerestory, and no air except through one or two broken panes.

Sometimes, lying on my divan, and looking out through the vermilion doors, I used to surprise a pair of swallows dropping down from their nest in the cedar-beams to preen themselves on the fountain's edge or in the channels of the pavement; for the roof was full of birds who came and went through the broken panes of the clerestory. Usually they were my only visitors; but one morning just at daylight I was waked by a soft tramp of bare feet, and saw, silhouetted against the cream-coloured walls, a procession of eight tall negroes in linen

From a photograph taken by Mme. la Marquise de Segonzac

Marrakech—apartment of the grand vizier's favorite, Palace of the Bahia

tunics, who filed noiselessly across the atrium like a moving frieze of bronze. In that fantastic setting, and the hush of that twilight hour, the vision was so like the picture of a "Seraglio Tragedy," some fragment of a Delacroix or Decamps floating up into the drowsy brain, that I almost fancied I had seen the ghosts of Ba-Ahmed's executioners revisiting with dagger and bowstring the scene of an unavenged crime.

A cock crew, and they vanished . . . and when I made the mistake of asking what they had been doing in my room at that hour I was told (as though it were the most natural thing in the world) that they were the municipal lamp-lighters of Marrakech, whose duty it is to refill every morning the two hundred acetylene lamps lighting the palace of the Resident General. Such unforeseen aspects, in this mysterious city, do the most ordinary domestic functions wear.

MARRAKECH

III

THE BAZAARS

PASSING out of the enchanted circle of the Bahia it
is startling to plunge into the native life about its
gates.

Marrakech is the great market of the south; and
the south means not only the Atlas with its feudal
chiefs and their wild clansmen, but all that lies
beyond of heat and savagery: the Sahara of the
veiled Touaregs, Dakka, Timbuctoo, Senegal and
the Soudan. Here come the camel caravans from
Demnat and Tameslout, from the Moulouya and
the Souss, and those from the Atlantic ports and
the confines of Algeria. The population of this
old city of the southern march has always been
even more mixed than that of the northerly Moroccan towns. It is made up of the descendants of
all the peoples conquered by a long line of Sultans
who brought their trains of captives across the sea
from Moorish Spain and across the Sahara from
Timbuctoo. Even in the highly cultivated region
on the lower slopes of the Atlas there are groups of
varied ethnic origin, the descendants of tribes

transplanted by long-gone rulers and still preserving many of their original characteristics.

In the bazaars all these peoples meet and mingle: cattle-dealers, olive-growers, peasants from the Atlas, the Souss and the Draa, Blue Men of the Sahara, blacks from Senegal and the Soudan, coming in to trade with the wool-merchants, tanners, leather-merchants, silk-weavers, armourers, and makers of agricultural implements.

Dark, fierce and fanatical are these narrow *souks* of Marrakech. They are mere mud lanes roofed with rushes, as in South Tunisia and Timbuctoo, and the crowds swarming in them are so dense that it is hardly possible, at certain hours, to approach the tiny raised kennels where the merchants sit like idols among their wares. One feels at once that something more than the thought of bargaining—dear as this is to the African heart—animates these incessantly moving throngs. The Souks of Marrakech seem, more than any others, the central organ of a native life that extends far beyond the city walls into secret clefts of the mountains and far-off oases where plots are hatched and holy wars fomented—farther still, to yellow deserts whence negroes are secretly brought across the Atlas to that inmost recess of the bazaar where the ancient traffic in flesh and blood still surreptitiously goes on.

All these many threads of the native life, woven of greed and lust, of fetichism and fear and blind hate of the stranger, form, in the *souks*, a thick network in which at times one's feet seem literally to stumble. Fanatics in sheepskins glowering from the guarded thresholds of the mosques, fierce tribesmen with inlaid arms in their belts and the fighters' tufts of wiry hair escaping from camel's-hair turbans, mad negroes standing stark naked in niches of the walls and pouring down Soudanese incantations upon the fascinated crowd, consumptive Jews with pathos and cunning in their large eyes and smiling lips, lusty slave-girls with earthen oil-jars resting against swaying hips, almond-eyed boys leading fat merchants by the hand, and bare-legged Berber women, tattooed and insolently gay, trading their striped blankets, or bags of dried roses and irises, for sugar, tea or Manchester cottons—from all these hundreds of unknown and unknowable people, bound together by secret affinities, or intriguing against each other with secret hate, there emanates an atmosphere of mystery and menace more stifling than the smell of camels and spices and black bodies and smoking fry which hangs like a fog under the close roofing of the *souks*.

And suddenly one leaves the crowd and the turbid air for one of those quiet corners that are like the back-waters of the bazaars: a small square where a vine stretches across a shop-front and hangs ripe clusters of grapes through the reeds. In the patterning of grape-shadows a very old donkey, tethered to a stone-post, dozes under a pack-saddle that is never taken off; and near by, in a matted niche, sits a very old man in white. This is the chief of the Guild of "morocco" workers of Marrakech, the most accomplished craftsman in Morocco in the preparing and using of the skins to which the city gives its name. Of these sleek moroccos, cream-white or dyed with cochineal or pomegranate skins, are made the rich bags of the Chleuh dancing-boys, the embroidered slippers for the harem, the belts and harnesses that figure so largely in Moroccan trade—and of the finest, in old days, were made the pomegranate-red morocco bindings of European bibliophiles.

From this peaceful corner one passes into the barbaric splendor of a *souk* hung with innumerable plumy bunches of floss silk—skeins of citron yellow, crimson, grasshopper green and pure purple. This is the silk-spinners' quarter, and next to it comes that of the dyers, with great seething vats into which the raw silk is plunged, and ropes overhead where the rainbow masses are hung out to dry.

Another turn leads into the street of the metal-workers and armourers, where the sunlight through the thatch flames on round flanks of beaten copper or picks out the silver bosses of ornate powder-flasks and pistols; and near by is the *souk* of the plough-shares, crowded with peasants in rough Chleuh cloaks who are waiting to have their archaic ploughs repaired, and that of the smiths, in an outer lane of mud huts where negroes squat in the dust and sinewy naked figures in tattered loin-cloths bend over blazing coals. And here ends the maze of the bazaars.

IV

THE AGDAL

ONE of the Almohad Sultans who, during their hundred years of empire, scattered such great monuments from Seville to the Atlas, felt the need of coolness about his southern capital, and laid out the olive-yards of the Agdal.

To the south of Marrakech the Agdal extends for many acres between the outer walls of the city and the edge of the palm-oasis—a continuous belt of silver foliage traversed by deep red lanes, and enclosing a wide-spreading summer palace and two immense reservoirs walled with masonry; and the vision of these serene sheets of water, in which the olives and palms are motionlessly reflected, is one of the most poetic impressions in that city of inveterate poetry.

On the edge of one of the reservoirs a sentimental Sultan built in the last century a little pleasure-house called the Menara. It is composed of a few rooms with a two-storied loggia looking across the water to the palm-groves, and surrounded by a garden of cypresses and orange-trees. The Menara, long since abandoned, is usually uninhabited; but on the day when we drove through the Agdal we noticed, at the gate, a group of well-dressed servants holding mules with embroidered saddle-clothes.

The French officer who was with us asked the porter what was going on, and he replied that the Chief of the Guild of Wool-Merchants had hired the pavilion for a week and invited a few friends to visit him. They were now, the porter added, taking tea in the loggia above the lake; and the host, being informed of our presence, begged that we should do him and his friends the honour of visiting the pavilion.

In reply to this amiable invitation we crossed an empty saloon surrounded with divans and passed out onto the loggia where the wool-merchant and his guests were seated. They were evidently persons of consequence: large bulky men wrapped in fresh muslins and reclining side by side on muslin-covered divans and cushions. Black slaves had placed before them brass trays with pots of mint-tea, glasses in filigree stands, and dishes of gazelles' horns and sugar-plums; and they sat serenely ab-

sorbing these refreshments and gazing with large
calm eyes upon the motionless water and the reflected trees.

So, we were told, they would probably spend the
greater part of their holiday. The merchant's
cooks had taken possession of the kitchens, and
toward sunset a sumptuous repast of many courses
would be carried into the saloon on covered trays,
and the guests would squat about it on rugs of
Rabat, tearing with their fingers the tender chicken
wings and small artichokes cooked in oil, plunging
their fat white hands to the wrist into huge mounds
of saffron and rice, and washing off the traces of
each course in the brass basin of perfumed water
carried about by a young black slave-girl with hoop-
earrings and a green-and-gold scarf about her hips.

Then the singing-girls would come out from Marrakech, squat round-faced young women heavily
hennaed and bejewelled, accompanied by gaunt
musicians in bright caftans; and for hours they
would sing sentimental or obscene ballads to the
persistent maddening twang of violin and flute and
drum. Meanwhile fiery brandy or sweet cham-
pagne would probably be passed around between

the steaming glasses of mint-tea which the slaves
perpetually refilled; or perhaps the sultry air, the
heavy meal, the scent of the garden and the vertig-
inous repetition of the music would suffice to
plunge these sedentary worthies into the delicious
coma in which every festive evening in Morocco
ends.

The next day would be spent in the same manner,
except that probably the Chleuh boys with sidelong
eyes and clean caftans would come instead of the
singing-girls, and weave the arabesque of their
dance in place of the runic pattern of the singing.
But the result would always be the same: a prolonged .state of obese ecstasy culminating in the
collapse of huge heaps of snoring muslin on the
divans against the wall. Finally at the week's end
the wool-merchant and his friends would all ride
back with dignity to the bazaar.

MARRAKECH

V

ON THE ROOFS

"SHOULD you like to see the Chleuh boys dance?" some one asked.

"There they are," another of our companions added, pointing to a dense ring of spectators on one side of the immense dusty square at the entrance of the *souks*—the "Square of the Dead" as it is called, in memory of the executions that used to take place under one of its grim red gates.

It is the square of the living now, the centre of all the life, amusement and gossip of Marrakech, and the spectators are so thickly packed about the story-tellers, snake-charmers and dancers who frequent it that one can guess what is going on within each circle only by the wailing monologue or the persistent drum-beat that proceeds from it.

Ah, yes—we should indeed like to see the Chleuh boys dance; we who, since we had been in Morocco, had seen no dancing, heard no singing, caught no single glimpse of merry-making! But how were we to get within sight of them?

On one side of the "Square of the Dead" stands

a large house, of European build, but modelled on Oriental lines: the office of the French municipal administration. The French Government no longer allows its offices to be built within the walls of Moroccan towns, and this house goes back to the epic days of the Caïd Sir Harry Maclean, to whom it was presented by the fantastic Abd-el-Aziz when the Caïd was his favourite companion as well as his military adviser.

At the suggestion of the municipal officials we mounted the stairs and looked down on the packed square. There can be no more Oriental sight this side of the Atlas and the Sahara. The square is surrounded by low mud-houses, fondaks, cafés, and the like. In one corner, near the archway leading into the *souks*, is the fruit-market, where the red-gold branches of unripe dates* for animal fodder are piled up in great stacks, and dozens of donkeys are coming and going, their panniers laden with fruits and vegetables which are being heaped on the ground in gorgeous pyramids: purple egg-plants, melons, cucumbers, bright orange pumpkins, mauve and pink and violet onions, rusty crimson pome-

* Dates do not ripen in Morocco.

From a photograph from "France-Maroc"

Marrakech—a fondak

granates and the gold grapes of Sefrou and Salé, all mingled with fresh green sheaves of mint and wormwood.

In the middle of the square sit the story-tellers' turbaned audiences. Beyond these are the humbler crowds about the wild-ringleted snake-charmers with their epileptic gestures and hissing incantations, and farther off, in the densest circle of all, we could just discern the shaved heads and waving surpliced arms of the dancing-boys. Under an archway near by an important personage in white muslin, mounted on a handsome mule and surrounded by his attendants, sat with motionless face and narrowed eyes gravely following the movements of the dancers.

Suddenly, as we stood watching the extraordinary animation of the scene, a reddish light overspread it, and one of our companions exclaimed: "Ah—a dust-storm!"

In that very moment it was upon us: a red cloud rushing across the square out of nowhere, whirling the date-branches over the heads of the squatting throngs, tumbling down the stacks of fruits and vegetables, rooting up the canvas awnings over the lemonade-sellers' stalls and before the café doors, huddling the blinded donkeys under the walls of the fondak, and stripping to the hips the black slave-girls scudding home from the *souks*.

Such a blast would instantly have scattered any western crowd, but "the patient East" remained undisturbed, rounding its shoulders before the storm and continuing to follow attentively the motions of the dancers and the turns of the story-tellers. By and bye, however, the gale grew too furious, and the spectators were so involved in collapsing tents, eddying date-branches and stampeding mules that the square began to clear, save for the listeners about the most popular story-teller, who continued to sit on unmoved. And then, at the height of the storm, they too were abruptly scattered by the rush of a cavalcade across the square. First came a handsomely dressed man, carrying before him on his peaked saddle a tiny boy in a gold-embroidered orange caftan, in front of whom he held an open book; and behind them a train of white-draped men on showily harnessed mules, followed by musicians in bright dresses. It was only a Circumcision procession on its way to the mosque; but the dust-enveloped rider in his rich dress, clutching the bewildered child to his breast, looked like some Oriental prince trying to escape with his son from the fiery embraces of desert Erl-maidens.

As swiftly as it rose the storm subsided, leaving the fruit-market in ruins under a sky as clear and innocent as an infant's eye. The Chleuh boys had vanished with the rest, like marionettes swept into a drawer by an impatient child; but presently, toward sunset, we were told that we were to see them after all, and our hosts led us up to the roof of the Caïd's house.

The city lay stretched before us like one immense terrace circumscribed by palms. The sky was pure blue, verging to turquoise green where the Atlas floated above mist; and facing the celestial snows stood the Koutoubya, red in the sunset.

People were beginning to come out on the roofs: it was the hour of peace, of ablutions, of family life on the house-tops. Groups of women in pale tints and floating veils spoke to each other from terrace to terrace, through the chatter of children and the guttural calls of bedizened negresses. And presently, on the roof adjoining ours, appeared the slim dancing-boys with white caftans and hennaed feet.

The three swarthy musicians who accompanied them crossed their lean legs on the tiles and set up their throb-throb and thrum-thrum, and on a narrow strip of terrace the youths began their measured steps.

It was a grave static dance, such as David may have performed before the Ark; untouched by mirth or folly, as beseemed a dance in that sombre land, and borrowing its magic from its gravity. Even when the pace quickened with the stress of the music the gestures still continued to be restrained and hieratic; only when, one by one, the performers detached themselves from the round and knelt before us for the *peseta* it is customary to press on their foreheads, did one see, by the moisture which made the coin adhere, how quick and violent their movements had been.

The performance, like all things Oriental, like the life, the patterns, the stories, seemed to have no beginning and no end: it just went monotonously and indefatigably on till fate snipped its thread by calling us away to dinner. And so at last we went

down into the dust of the streets refreshed by that
vision of white youths dancing on the house-tops
against the gold of a sunset that made them look—
in spite of ankle-bracelets and painted eyes—almost
as guileless and happy as the round of angels on the
roof of Fra Angelico's Nativity.

VI

THE SAADIAN TOMBS

ON one of the last days of our stay in Marrakech
we were told, almost mysteriously, that permission
was to be given us to visit the tombs of the Saadian
Sultans.

Though Marrakech has been in the hands of the
French since 1912, the very existence of these tombs
was unknown to the authorities till 1917. Then
the Sultan's government privately informed the
Resident General that an unsuspected treasure of
Moroccan art was falling into ruin, and after some
hesitation it was agreed that General Lyautey and
the Director of Fine Arts should be admitted to
the mosque containing the tombs, on the express
condition that the French Government undertook

to repair them. While we were at Rabat General Lyautey had described his visit to us, and it was at his request that the Sultan authorized us to see the mosque, to which no travellers had as yet been admitted.

With a good deal of ceremony, and after the customary *pourparlers* with the great Pasha who controls native affairs at Marrakech, an hour was fixed for our visit, and we drove through long lanes of mud-huts to a lost quarter near the walls. At last we came to a deserted square on one side of which stands the long low mosque of Mansourah with a turquoise-green minaret embroidered with traceries of sculptured terra cotta. Opposite the mosque is a gate in a crumbling wall; and at this gate the Pasha's Cadi was to meet us with the keys of the mausoleum. But we waited in vain. Oriental dilatoriness, or a last secret reluctance to admit unbelievers to a holy place, had caused the Cadi to forget his appointment; and we drove away disappointed.

The delay drove us to wondering about these mysterious Saadian Sultans, who, though coming so late in the annals of Morocco, had left at least one monument said to be worthy of the Merinid tradition. And the tale of the Saadians is worth telling.

They came from Arabia to the Draa (the fruitful country south of the Great Atlas) early in the fifteenth century, when the Merinid empire was already near disintegration. Like all previous invaders they preached the doctrine of a pure Islamism to the polytheistic and indifferent Berbers, and found a ready hearing because they denounced the evils of a divided empire, and also because the whole of Morocco was in revolt against the Christian colonies of Spain and Portugal, which had encircled the coast from Ceuta to Agadir with a chain of fortified counting-houses. To *bouter dehors* the money-making unbeliever was an object that found adherents from the Rif to the Sahara, and the Saadian cherifs soon rallied a mighty following to their standard. Islam, though it never really gave a creed to the Berbers, supplied them with a war-cry as potent to-day as when it first rang across Barbary.

The history of the Saadians is a foreshortened record of that of all their predecessors. They over-

threw the artistic and luxurious Merinids, and in
their turn became artistic and luxurious. Their
greatest Sultan, Abou-el-Abbas, surnamed "The
Golden," after defeating the Merinids and putting
an end to Christian rule in Morocco by the crush-
ing victory of El-Ksar (1578), bethought him in his
turn of enriching himself and beautifying his capital,
and with this object in view turned his attention to
the black kingdoms of the south.

Senegal and the Soudan, which had been Moham-
medan since the eleventh century, had attained in
the sixteenth century a high degree of commercial
wealth and artistic civilization. The Sultanate of
Timbuctoo seems in reality to have been a thriving
empire, and if Timbuctoo was not the Claude-like
vision of Carthaginian palaces which it became in
the tales of imaginative travellers, it apparently
had something of the magnificence of Fez and Marrakech.

The Saadian army, after a march of four and a
half months across the Sahara, conquered the whole
black south. Senegal, the Soudan and Bornou submitted to Abou-el-Abbas, the Sultan of Timbuctoo
was dethroned, and the celebrated negro jurist
Ahmed-Baba was brought a prisoner to Marrakech,

where his chief sorrow appears to have been for the loss of his library of 1,600 volumes—though he declared that, of all the numerous members of his family, it was he who possessed the smallest number of books.

Besides this learned bibliophile, the Sultan Abou-el-Abbas brought back with him an immense booty, principally of ingots of gold, from which he took his surname of "The Golden"; and as the result of the expedition Marrakech was embellished with mosques and palaces for which the Sultan brought marble from Carrara, paying for it with loaves of sugar from the sugar-cane that the Saadians grew in the Souss.

In spite of these brilliant beginnings the rule of the dynasty was short and without subsequent interest. Based on a fanatical antagonism against the foreigner, and fed by the ever-wakeful hatred of the Moors for their Spanish conquerors, it raised ever higher the Chinese walls of exclusiveness which the more enlightened Almohads and Merinids had sought to overthrow. Henceforward less and less daylight and fresh air were to penetrate into the *souks* of Morocco.

The day after our unsuccessful attempt to see

the tombs of these ephemeral rulers we received another message, naming an hour for our visit; and this time the Pasha's representative was waiting in the archway. We followed his lead, under the openly mistrustful glances of the Arabs who hung about the square, and after picking our way through a twisting land between walls we came out into a filthy nettle-grown space against the ramparts. At intervals of about thirty feet splendid square towers rose from the walls, and facing one of them lay a group of crumbling buildings masked behind other ruins.

We were led first into a narrow mosque or praying-chapel, like those of the Medersas, with a coffered cedar ceiling resting on four marble columns, and traceried walls of unusually beautiful design. From this chapel we passed into the hall of the tombs, a cube about forty feet square. Fourteen columns of colored marble sustain a domed ceiling of gilded cedar, with an exterior deambulatory under a tunnel-vaulting also roofed with cedar. The walls are, as usual, of chiselled stucco, above revêtements of ceramic mosaic, and between the columns lie the white marble cenotaphs of the

Saadian Sultans, covered with Arabic inscriptions in the most delicate low-relief. Beyond this central mausoleum, and balancing the praying-chapel, lies another long narrow chamber, gold-ceilinged also, and containing a few tombs.

It is difficult, in describing the architecture of Morocco, to avoid producing an impression of monotony. The ground-plan of mosques and Medersas is always practically the same; and the same elements, few in number and endlessly repeated, make up the materials and the form of the ornament. The effect upon the eye is not monotonous, for a patient art has infinitely varied the combinations of pattern and the juxtapositions of color; while the depth of undercutting of the stucco, and the treatment of the bronze doors and of the carved cedar corbels, necessarily varies with the periods which produced them.

But in the Saadian mausoleum a new element has been introduced which makes this little monument a thing apart. The marble columns supporting the roof appear to be unique in Moroccan architecture, and they lend themselves to a new roof-plan which relates the building rather to the tradition of Venice or Byzantine by way of Kairouan and Cordova.

The late date of the monument precludes any idea of a direct artistic tradition. The most probable explanation seems to be that the architect of the mausoleum was familiar with European Renaissance architecture, and saw the beauty to be derived from using precious marbles not merely as ornament, but in the Roman and Italian way, as a structural element. Panels and fountain-basins are ornament, and ornament changes nothing essential in architecture; but when, for instance, heavy square piers are replaced by detached columns, a new style results.

It is not only the novelty of its plan that makes the Saadian mausoleum singular among Moroccan monuments. The details of its ornament are of the most intricate refinement: it seems as though the last graces of the expiring Merinid art had been gathered up into this rare blossom. And the slant of sunlight on lustrous columns, the depths of fretted gold, the dusky ivory of the walls and the pure white of the cenotaphs, so classic in spareness of ornament and simplicity of design—this subtle

From a photograph by M. André Chevrillon

Marrakech—Mausoleum of the Saadian Sultans (sixteenth century) showing the tombs

harmony of form and color gives to the dim rich chapel an air of dream-like unreality.

And how can it seem other than a dream? Who can have conceived, in the heart of a savage Saharan camp, the serenity and balance of this hidden place? And how came such fragile loveliness to survive, preserving, behind a screen of tumbling walls, of nettles and offal and dead beasts, every curve of its traceries and every cell of its honey-combing?

Such questions inevitably bring one back to the central riddle of the mysterious North African civilization: the perpetual flux and the immovable stability, the barbarous customs and sensuous refinements, the absence of artistic originality and the gift for regrouping borrowed motives, the patient and exquisite workmanship and the immediate neglect and degradation of the thing once made.

Revering the dead and camping on their graves, elaborating exquisite monuments only to abandon and defile them, venerating scholarship and wisdom and living in ignorance and grossness, these gifted races, perpetually struggling to reach some higher level of culture from which they have always been swept down by a fresh wave of barbarism, are still only a people in the making.

It may be that the political stability which France is helping them to acquire will at last give their higher qualities time for fruition; and when one looks at the mausoleum of Marrakech and the Medersas of Fez one feels that, were the experiment made on artistic grounds alone, it would yet be well worth making.

V

HAREMS AND CEREMONIES

V

HAREMS AND CEREMONIES

I

THE CROWD IN THE STREET

TO occidental travellers the most vivid impression produced by a first contact with the Near East is the surprise of being in a country where the human element increases instead of diminishing the delight of the eye.

After all, then, the intimate harmony between nature and architecture and the human body that is revealed in Greek art was not an artist's counsel of perfection but an honest rendering of reality: there were, there still are, privileged scenes where the fall of a green-grocer's draperies or a milkman's cloak or a beggar's rags are part of the composition, distinctly related to it in line and colour, and where the natural unstudied attitudes of the human body are correspondingly harmonious, however hum-

[161]

drum the acts it is engaged in. The discovery, to the traveller returning from the East, robs the most romantic scenes of western Europe of half their charm: in the Piazza of San Marco, in the market-place of Siena, where at least the robes of the Procurators or the gay tights of Pinturic-chio's striplings once justified man's presence among his works, one can see, at first, only the outrage inflicted on beauty by the "plentiful strutting manikins" of the modern world.

Moroccan crowds are always a feast to the eye. The instinct of skilful drapery, the sense of colour (subdued by custom, but breaking out in subtle glimpses under the universal ashy tints) make the humblest assemblage of donkey-men and water-carriers an ever-renewed delight. But it is only on rare occasions, and in the court ceremonies to which so few foreigners have had access, that the hidden sumptuousness of the native life is revealed. Even then, the term sumptuousness may seem ill-chosen, since the nomadic nature of African life persists in spite of palaces and chamberlains and all the elaborate ritual of the Makhzen, and the most pompous rites are likely to end in a dusty gallop of wild tribesmen, and the most princely processions to tail off in a string of half-naked urchins riding bareback on donkeys.

As in all Oriental countries, the contact between prince and beggar, vizier and serf is disconcertingly free and familiar, and one must see the highest court officials kissing the hem of the Sultan's robe, and hear authentic tales of slaves given by one merchant to another at the end of a convivial evening, to be reminded that nothing is as democratic in appearance as a society of which the whole structure hangs on the whim of one man.

II

AÏD-EL-KEBIR

In the verandah of the Residence of Rabat I stood looking out between posts festooned with gentian-blue ipomeas at the first shimmer of light on black cypresses and white tobacco-flowers, on the scattered roofs of the new town, and the plain stretching away to the Sultan's palace above the sea.

We had been told, late the night before, that the Sultan would allow Madame Lyautey, with the three ladies of her party, to be present at the great religious rite of the Aïd-el-Kebir (the Sacrifice of the Sheep). The honour was an unprecedented one, a favour probably conceded only at the last moment: for as a rule no women are admitted to these ceremonies. It was an opportunity not to be missed; and all through the short stifling night I had lain awake wondering if I should be ready early enough. Presently the motors assembled, and we set out with the French officers in attendance on the Governor's wife.

The Sultan's palace, a large modern building on the familiar Arab lines, lies in a treeless and gardenless waste enclosed by high walls and close above the blue Atlantic. We motored past the gates, where the Sultan's Black Guard was drawn up, and out to the *msalla*,* a sort of common adjacent to all the Sultan's residences where public ceremonies are usually performed. The sun was already beating down on the great plain thronged with horsemen and with the native population of Rabat on mule-back and foot. Within an open

* The *msalla* is used for the performance of religious ceremonies when the crowd is too great to be contained in the court of the mosque.

space in the centre of the crowd a canvas palissade dyed with a bold black pattern surrounded‧ the Sultan's tents. The Black Guard, in scarlet tunics and white and green turbans, were drawn up on the edge of the open space, keeping the spectators at a distance; but under the guidance of our companions we penetrated to the edge of the crowd.

The palissade was open on one side, and within it we could see moving about among the snowy-robed officials a group of men in straight narrow gowns of almond-green, peach-blossom, lilac and pink; they were the Sultan's musicians, whose coloured dresses always flower out conspicuously among the white draperies of all the other court attendants.

In the tent nearest the opening, against a background of embroidered hangings, a circle of majestic turbaned old men squatted placidly on Rabat rugs. Presently the circle broke up, there was an agitated coming and going, and some one said: "The Sultan has gone to the tent at the back of the enclosure to kill the sheep."

A sense of the impending solemnity ran through the crowd. The mysterious rumour which is the

Voice of the Bazaar rose about us like the wind
in a palm-oasis; the Black Guard fired a salute
from an adjoining hillock; the clouds of red dust
flung up by wheeling horsemen thickened and then
parted, and a white-robed rider sprang out from
the tent of the Sacrifice with something red and
dripping across his saddle-bow, and galloped away
toward Rabat through the shouting. A little
shiver ran over the group of occidental spectators,
who knew that the dripping red thing was a sheep
with its throat so skilfully slit that, if the omen
were favourable, it would live on through the long
race to Rabat and gasp out its agonized life on the
tiles of the Mosque.

The Sacrifice of the Sheep, one of the four great
Moslem rites, is simply the annual propitiatory
offering made by every Mahometan head of a
family, and by the Sultan as such. It is based not
on a Koranic injunction, but on the "Souna" or
record of the Prophet's "custom" or usages, which
forms an authoritative precedent in Moslem ritual.
So far goes the Moslem exegesis. In reality, of
course, the Moslem blood-sacrifice comes, by way
of the Semitic ritual, from far beyond and behind

it; and the belief that the Sultan's prosperity for
the coming year depends on the animal's protracted
agony seems to relate the ceremony to the dark
magic so deeply rooted in the mysterious tribes
peopling North Africa long ages before the first
Phoenician prows had rounded its coast.

Between the Black Guard and the tents, five
or six horses were being led up and down by muscular grooms in snowy tunics. They were handsome animals, as Moroccan horses go, and each
of a different colour; and on the bay horse was
a red saddle embroidered in gold, on the piebald
a saddle of peach-colour and silver, on the chestnut, grass-green encrusted with seed-pearls, on
the white mare purple housings, and orange velvet
on the grey. The Sultan's band had struck up
a shrill hammering and twanging, the salute of
the Black Guard continued at intervals, and the
caparisoned steeds began to rear and snort and
drag back from the cruel Arab bits with their exquisite *niello* incrustations. Some one whispered
that these were His Majesty's horses—and that
it was never known till he appeared which one he
would mount.

Presently the crowd about the tents thickened, and when it divided again there emerged from it a grey horse bearing a motionless figure swathed in blinding white. Marching at the horse's bridle, lean brown grooms in white tunics rhythmically waved long strips of white linen to keep off the flies from the Imperial Presence; and beside the motionless rider, in a line with his horse's flank, rode the Imperial Parasol-bearer, who held above the sovereign's head a great sunshade of bright green velvet. Slowly the grey horse advanced a few yards before the tent; behind rode the court dignitaries, followed by the musicians, who looked, in their bright scant caftans, like the slender music-making angels of a Florentine fresco.

The Sultan, pausing beneath his velvet dome, waited to receive the homage of the assembled tribes. An official, riding forward, drew bridle and called out a name. Instantly there came storming across the plain a wild cavalcade of tribesmen, with rifles slung across their shoulders, pistols and cutlasses in their belts, and twists of camel's-hair bound about their turbans. Within a few feet of the Sultan they drew in, their leader

The Sultan of Morocco under the green umbrella (at Meknez. 1916)

uttered a cry and sprang forward, bending to the saddle-bow, and with a great shout the tribe galloped by, each man bowed over his horse's neck as he flew past the hieratic figure on the grey horse.

Again and again this ceremony was repeated, the Sultan advancing a few feet as each new group thundered toward him. There were more than ten thousand horsemen and chieftains from the Atlas and the wilderness, and as the ceremony continued the dust-clouds grew denser and more fiery-golden, till at last the forward-surging lines showed through them like blurred images in a tarnished mirror.

As the Sultan advanced we followed, abreast of him and facing the oncoming squadrons. The contrast between his motionless figure and the wild waves of cavalry beating against it typified the strange soul of Islam, with its impetuosity forever culminating in impassiveness. The sun hung high, a brazen ball in a white sky, darting down metallic shafts on the dust-enveloped plain and the serene white figure under its umbrella. The fat man with a soft round beard-fringed face, wrapped in spirals of pure white, one plump hand on his embroidered bridle, his yellow-slippered feet thrust heel-down in big velvet-lined stirrups, became, through sheer immobility, a symbol, a mystery, a God. The human flux beat against him, dissolved, ebbed away, another spear-crested wave swept up behind it and dissolved in turn; and he sat on, hour after hour, under the white-hot sky, unconscious of the heat, the dust, the tumult, embodying to the wild factious precipitate hordes a long tradition of serene aloofness.

III

THE IMPERIAL MIRADOR

As the last riders galloped up to do homage we were summoned to our motors and driven rapidly to the palace. The Sultan had sent word to Mme. Lyautey that the ladies of the Imperial harem would entertain her and her guests while his Majesty received the Resident General, and we had to hasten back in order not to miss the next act of the spectacle.

We walked across a long court lined with the Black Guard, passed under a gateway, and were

From a photograph from "France-Maroc"

A clan of mountaineers and their caïd

met by a shabbily dressed negress. Traversing a hot dazzle of polychrome tiles we reached another archway guarded by the chief eunuch, a towering black with the enamelled eyes of a basalt bust. The eunuch delivered us to other negresses, and we entered a labyrinth of inner passages and patios, all murmuring and dripping with water. Passing down long corridors where slaves in dim greyish garments flattened themselves against the walls, we caught glimpses of great dark rooms, laundries, pantries, bakeries, kitchens, where savoury things were brewing and stewing, and where more negresses, abandoning their pots and pans, came to peep at us from the threshold. In one corner, on a bench against a wall hung with matting, grey parrots in tall cages were being fed by a slave.

A narrow staircase mounted to a landing where a princess out of an Arab fairy-tale awaited us. Stepping softly on her embroidered slippers she led us to the next landing, where another golden-slippered being smiled out on us, a little girl this one, blushing and dimpling under a jewelled diadem and pearl-woven braids. On a third landing a third damsel appeared, and encircled by the three

[171]

graces we mounted to the tall *mirador* in the central tower from which we were to look down at the coming ceremony. One by one, our little guides, kicking off their golden shoes, which a slave laid neatly outside the door, led us on soft bare feet into the upper chamber of the harem.

It was a large room, enclosed on all sides by a balcony glazed with panes of brightly-coloured glass. On a gaudy modern Rabat carpet stood gilt armchairs of florid design and a table bearing a commercial bronze of the "art goods" variety. Divans with muslin-covered cushions were ranged against the walls and down an adjoining gallery-like apartment which was otherwise furnished only with clocks. The passion for clocks and other mechanical contrivances is common to all unmechanical races, and every chief's palace in North Africa contains a collection of time-pieces which might be called striking if so many had not ceased to go. But those in the Sultan's harem of Rabat are remarkable for the fact that, while designed on current European models, they are proportioned in size to the Imperial dignity, so that a Dutch "grandfather" becomes a wardrobe, and the box-

clock of the European mantelpiece a cupboard that
has to be set on the floor. At the end of this
avenue of time-pieces a European double-bed with
a bright silk quilt covered with Nottingham lace
stood majestically on a carpeted platform.

But for the enchanting glimpses of sea and plain
through the lattices of the gallery, the apartment of
the Sultan's ladies falls far short of occidental ideas
of elegance. But there was hardly time to think
of this, for the door of the *mirador* was always opening to let in another fairy-tale figure, till at last
we were surrounded by a dozen houris, laughing,
babbling, taking us by the hand, and putting shy
questions while they looked at us with caressing
eyes. They were all (our interpretess whispered)
the Sultan's "favourites," round-faced apricot-
tinted girls in their teens, with high cheek-bones,
full red lips, surprised brown eyes between curved-
up Asiatic lids, and little brown hands fluttering
out like birds from their brocaded sleeves.

In honour of the ceremony, and of Mme.
Lyautey's visit, they had put on their finest
clothes, and their freedom of movement was somewhat hampered by their narrow sumptuous gowns,

with over-draperies of gold and silver brocade and pale rosy gauze held in by corset-like sashes of gold tissue of Fez, and the heavy silken cords that looped their voluminous sleeves. Above their foreheads the hair was shaven like that of an Italian fourteenth-century beauty, and only a black line as narrow as a pencilled eyebrow showed through the twist of gauze fastened by a jewelled clasp above the real eye-brows. Over the forehead-jewel rose the complicated structure of the head-dress. Ropes of black wool were plaited through the hair, forming, at the back, a double loop that stood out above the nape like the twin handles of a vase, the upper veiled in airy shot gauzes and fastened with jewelled bands and ornaments. On each side of the red cheeks other braids were looped over the ears hung with broad earrings of filigree set with rough pearls and emeralds, or gold hoops and pendants of coral; and an unexpected tulle ruff, like that of a Watteau shepherdess, framed the round chin above a torrent of necklaces, necklaces of amber, coral, baroque pearls, hung with mysterious barbaric amulets and fetiches. As the young things moved about us on soft hennaed feet the light played on shifting gleams of gold and silver, blue and violet and apple-green, all harmonized and bemisted by clouds of pink and sky-blue; and through the changing group capered a little black picaninny in a caftan of silver-shot purple with a sash of raspberry red.

But presently there was a flutter in the aviary. A fresh pair of *babouches* clicked on the landing, and a young girl, less brilliantly dressed and less brilliant of face than the others, came in on bare painted feet. Her movements were shy and hesitating, her large lips pale, her eye-brows less vividly dark, her head less jewelled. But all the little humming-birds gathered about her with respectful rustlings as she advanced toward us leaning on one of the young girls, and holding out her ringed hand to Mme. Lyautey's curtsey. It was the young Princess, the Sultan's legitimate daughter. She examined us with sad eyes, spoke a few compliments through the interpretess, and seated herself in silence, letting the others sparkle and chatter.

Conversation with the shy Princess was flagging when one of the favourites beckoned us to the balcony. We were told we might push open the painted panes a few inches, but as we did so the butterfly group drew back lest they should be seen looking out on the forbidden world.

Salutes were crashing out again from the direction of the *msalla:* puffs of smoke floated over the slopes like thistle-down. Farther off, a pall of red vapour veiled the gallop of the last horsemen wheeling away toward Rabat. The vapour subsided, and moving out of it we discerned a slow procession. First rode a detachment of the Black Guard, mounted on black horses, and, comically fierce in their British scarlet and Meccan green, a uniform invented at the beginning of the nineteenth century by a retired English army officer. After the Guard came the standard-bearers and the great dignitaries, then the Sultan, still aloof, immovable, as if rapt in the contemplation of his mystic office. More court officials followed, then the bright-gowned musicians on foot, then a confused irrepressible crowd of pilgrims, beggars, saints, mountebanks, and the other small folk of the Bazaar, ending in a line of boys jamming their naked heels into the ribs of world-weary donkeys.

The Sultan rode into the court below us, and

From a photograph from "France-Maroc"

The Sultan entering Marrakech in state

Vizier and chamberlains, snowy-white against the scarlet line of the Guards, hurried forward to kiss his draperies, his shoes, his stirrup. Descending from his velvet saddle, still entranced, he paced across the tiles between a double line of white servitors bowing to the ground. White pigeons circled over him like petals loosed from a great orchard, and he disappeared with his retinue under the shadowy arcade of the audience chamber at the back of the court.

At this point one of the favourites called us in from the *mirador*. The door had just opened to admit an elderly woman preceded by a respectful group of girls. From the newcomer's round ruddy face, her short round body, the round hands emerging from her round wrists, an inexplicable majesty emanated; and though she too was less richly arrayed than the favourites she carried her head-dress of striped gauze like a crown.

This impressive old lady was the Sultan's mother. As she held out her plump wrinkled hand to Mme. Lyautey and spoke a few words through the interpretess one felt that at last a painted window of the *mirador* had been broken, and a thought let into the vacuum of the harem. What thought, it would have taken deep insight into the processes of the Arab mind to discover; but its honesty was manifest in the old Empress's voice and smile. Here at last was a woman beyond the trivial dissimulations, the childish cunning, the idle cruelties of the harem. It was not a surprise to be told that she was her son's most trusted adviser, and the chief authority in the palace. If such a woman deceived and intrigued it would be for great purposes and for ends she believed in: the depth of her soul had air and daylight in it, and she would never willingly shut them out.

The Empress Mother chatted for a while with Mme. Lyautey, asking about the Resident General's health, enquiring for news of the war, and saying, with an emotion perceptible even through the unintelligible words: "All is well with Morocco as long as all is well with France." Then she withdrew, and we were summoned again to the *mirador*.

This time it was to see a company of officers in brilliant uniforms advancing at a trot across the plain from Rabat. At sight of the figure that

headed them, so slim, erect and young on his splendid chestnut, with a pale blue tunic barred by the
wide orange ribbon of the Cherifian Order, salutes
pealed forth again from the slope above the palace
and the Black Guard presented arms. A moment
later General Lyautey and his staff were riding
in at the gates below us. On the threshold of the
inner court they dismounted, and moving to the
other side of our balcony we followed the next
stage of the ceremony. The Sultan was still seated
in the audience chamber. The court officials still
stood drawn up in a snow-white line against the
snow-white walls. The great dignitaries advanced
across the tiles to greet the General; then they
fell aside, and he went forward alone, followed at
a little distance by his staff. A third of the way
across the court he paused, in accordance with
the Moroccan court ceremonial, and bowed in the
direction of the arcaded room; a few steps farther
he bowed again, and a third time on the threshold
of the room. Then French uniforms and Moroccan
draperies closed in about him, and all vanished into
the shadows of the audience hall.

Our audience too seemed to be over. We had

exhausted the limited small talk of the harem, had learned from the young beauties that, though they were forbidden to look on at the ceremony, the dancers and singers would come to entertain them presently, and had begun to take leave when a negress hurried in to say that his Majesty begged Mme. Lyautey and her friends to await his arrival. This was the crowning incident of our visit, and I wondered with what Byzantine ritual the Anointed One fresh from the exercise of his priestly functions would be received among his women.

The door opened, and without any announcement or other preliminary flourish a fat man with a pleasant face, his djellabah stretched over a portly front, walked in holding a little boy by the hand. Such was his Majesty the Sultan Moulay Youssef, despoiled of sacramental burnouses and turban, and shuffling along on bare yellow-slippered feet with the gait of a stout elderly gentleman who has taken off his boots in the passage preparatory to a domestic evening.

The little Prince, one of his two legitimate sons, was dressed with equal simplicity, for silken garments are worn in Morocco only by musicians,

boy-dancers and other hermaphrodite fry. With
his ceremonial raiment the Sultan had put off his
air of superhuman majesty, and the expression of
his round pale face corresponded with the plainness
of his dress. The favourites fluttered about him,
respectful but by no means awestruck, and the
youngest began to play with the little Prince. We
could well believe the report that his was the hap-
piest harem in Morocco, as well as the only one
into which a breath of the outer world ever came.

Moulay Youssef greeted Mme. Lyautey with
friendly simplicity, made the proper speeches to
her companions, and then, with the air of the busi-
ness-man who has forgotten to give an order before leaving his office, he walked up to a corner of
the room, and while the flower-maidens ruffled
about him, and through the windows we saw the
last participants in the mystic rites galloping away
toward the crenellated walls of Rabat, his Majesty the Priest and Emperor of the Faithful unhooked a small instrument from the wall and applied his sacred lips to the telephone.

IV

IN OLD RABAT

BEFORE General Lyautey came to Morocco Rabat had been subjected to the indignity of European "improvements," and one must traverse boulevards scored with tram-lines, and pass between hotel-terraces and cafés and cinema-palaces, to reach the surviving nucleus of the once beautiful native town. Then, at the turn of a commonplace street, one comes upon it suddenly. The shops and cafés cease, the jingle of trams and the trumpeting of motor-horns die out, and here, all at once, are silence and solitude, and the dignified reticence of the windowless Arab house-fronts.

We were bound for the house of a high government official, a Moroccan dignitary of the old school, who had invited us to tea, and added a message to the effect that the ladies of his household would be happy to receive me.

The house we sought was some distance down the quietest of white-walled streets. Our companion knocked at a low green door, and we were admitted to a passage into which a wooden stairway descended. A brother-in-law of our host was waiting for us: in his wake we mounted the ladder-like stairs and entered a long room with a florid French carpet and a set of gilt furniture to match. There were no fretted walls, no painted cedar doors, no fountains rustling in unseen courts: the house was squeezed in between others, and such traces of old ornament as it may have possessed had vanished.

But presently we saw why its inhabitants were indifferent to such details. Our host, a handsome white-bearded old man, welcomed us in the doorway; then he led us to a raised oriel window at one end of the room, and seated us in the gilt armchairs face to face with one of the most beautiful views in Morocco.

Below us lay the white and blue terrace-roofs of the native town, with palms and minarets shooting up between them, or the shadows of a vine-trellis patterning a quiet lane. Beyond, the Atlantic sparkled, breaking into foam at the mouth of the Bou-Regreg and under the towering ramparts of the Kasbah of the Oudayas. To the right, the ruins of the great Mosque rose from their plateau over the river; and, on the farther side of the troubled flood, old Salé, white and wicked, lay like a jewel in its gardens. With such a scene beneath their eyes, the inhabitants of the house could hardly feel its lack of architectural interest.

After exchanging the usual compliments, and giving us time to enjoy the view, our host withdrew, taking with him the men of our party. A moment later he reappeared with a rosy fair-haired girl, dressed in Arab costume, but evidently of European birth. The brother-in-law explained that this young woman, who had "studied in Algeria," and whose mother was French, was the intimate friend of the ladies of the household, and would act as interpreter. Our host then again left us, joining the men visitors in another room, and the door opened to admit his wife and daughters-in-law.

The mistress of the house was a handsome Algerian with sad expressive eyes: the younger women were pale, fat and amiable. They all wore sober dresses, in keeping with the simplicity of the house, and but for the vacuity of their faces the group might have been that of a Professor's family in an English or American University town, decently costumed for an Arabian Nights' pageant in the college grounds. I was never more vividly reminded of the fact that human nature, from one pole to the other, falls naturally into certain categories, and that Respectability wears the same face in an Oriental harem as in England or America.

My hostesses received me with the utmost amiability, we seated ourselves in the oriel facing the view, and the interchange of questions and compliments began.

Had I any children? (They asked it all at once.)

Alas, no.

"In Islam" (one of the ladies ventured) "a woman without children is considered the most unhappy being in the world."

I replied that in the western world also childless women were pitied. (The brother-in-law smiled incredulously.)

Knowing that European fashions are of absorbing interest to the harem I next enquired: "What do these ladies think of our stiff tailor-dresses? Don't they find them excessively ugly?"

"Yes, they do;" (it was again the brother-in-law who replied.) "But they suppose that in your own homes you dress less badly."

"And have they never any desire to travel, or to visit the Bazaars, as the Turkish ladies do?"

"No, indeed. They are too busy to give such matters a thought. In *our country* women of the highest class occupy themselves with their household and their children, and the rest of their time is devoted to needlework." (At this statement I gave the brother-in-law a smile as incredulous as his own.)

All this time the fair-haired interpretess had not been allowed by the vigilant guardian of the harem to utter a word.

I turned to her with a question.

"So your mother is French, *Mademoiselle?*"

"*Oui, Madame.*"

"From what part of France did she come?"

A bewildered pause. Finally: "I don't know . . . from Switzerland, I think," brought out this shining example of the Higher Education. In spite of Algerian "advantages" the poor girl could speak only a few words of her mother's tongue. She had kept the European features and complexion, but her soul was the soul of Islam. The harem had placed its powerful imprint upon her, and she looked at me with the same remote and passive eyes as the daughters of the house.

After struggling for a while longer with a conversation which the watchful brother-in-law continued to direct as he pleased, I felt my own lips stiffening into the resigned smile of the harem, and it was a relief when at last their guardian drove the pale flock away, and the handsome old gentleman who owned them reappeared on the scene, bringing back my friends, and followed by slaves and tea.

V

IN FEZ

WHAT thoughts, what speculations, one wonders, go on under the narrow veiled brows of the little creatures destined to the high honour of marriage or concubinage in Moroccan palaces?

Some are brought down from mountains and cedar forests, from the free life of the tents where the nomad women go unveiled. Others come from harems in the turreted cities beyond the Atlas, where blue palm-groves beat all night against the stars and date-caravans journey across the desert from Timbuctoo. Some, born and bred in an airy palace among pomegranate gardens and white terraces, pass thence to one of the feudal fortresses near the snows, where for half the year the great chiefs of the south live in their clan, among fighting men and falconers and packs of *sloughis*. And still others grow up in a stifling Mellah, trip unveiled on its blue terraces overlooking the gardens of the great, and, seen one day at sunset by a fat vizier or his pale young master, are acquired for a handsome sum and transferred to the painted sepulchre of the harem.

Worst of all must be the fate of those who go from tents and cedar forests, or from some sea-blown garden above Rabat, into one of the houses of Old Fez. They are well-nigh impenetrable, these palaces of Elbali: the Fazi dignitaries do not welcome the visits of strange women. On the rare occasions when they are received, a member of the family (one of the sons, or a brother-in-law who has "studied in Algeria") usually acts as interpreter; and perhaps it is as well that no one from the outer world should come to remind these listless creatures that somewhere the gulls dance on the Atlantic and the wind murmurs through olive-yards and clatters the metallic fronds of palm-groves.

We had been invited, one day, to visit the harem of one of the chief dignitaries of the Makhzen at Fez, and these thoughts came to me as I sat among the pale women in their mouldering prison. The descent through the steep tunnelled streets gave one the sense of being lowered into the shaft of a mine. At each step the strip of sky grew narrower, and was more often obscured by the low vaulted passages into which we plunged. The noises of the Bazaar had died out, and only the sound of fountains behind garden walls and the clatter of our mules' hoofs on the stones went with us. Then fountains and gardens ceased also, the towering masonry closed in, and we entered an almost subterranean labyrinth which sun and air never reach. At length our mules turned into a *cul-de-sac* blocked by a high building. On the right was another building, one of those blind mysterious house-fronts of

Fez that seem like a fragment of its ancient fortifications. Clients and servants lounged on the
stone benches built into the wall; it was evidently
the house of an important person. A charming
youth with intelligent eyes waited on the threshold
to receive us: he was one of the sons of the house,
the one who had "studied in Algeria" and knew
how to talk to visitors. We followed him into a
small arcaded *patio* hemmed in by the high walls
of the house. On the right was the usual long room
with archways giving on the court. Our host, a
patriarchal personage, draped in fat as in a toga,
came toward us, a mountain of majestic muslins,
his eyes sparkling in a swarthy silver-bearded face.
He seated us on divans and lowered his voluminous
person to a heap of cushions on the step leading
into the court; and the son who had studied in
Algeria instructed a negress to prepare the tea.

Across the *patio* was another arcade closely hung
with unbleached cotton. From behind it came the
sound of chatter, and now and then a bare brown
child in a scant shirt would escape, and be hur-
riedly pulled back with soft explosions of laughter,
while a black woman came out to readjust the
curtains.

There were three of these negresses, splendid
bronze creatures, wearing white djellabahs over
bright-coloured caftans, striped scarves knotted
about their large hips, and gauze turbans on their
crinkled hair. Their wrists clinked with heavy
silver bracelets, and big circular earrings danced
in their purple ear-lobes. A languor lay on all the
other inmates of the household, on the servants
and hangers-on squatting in the shade under the
arcade, on our monumental host and his smiling
son; but the three negresses, vibrating with activity, rushed continually from the curtained chamber
to the kitchen, and from the kitchen to the master's
reception-room, bearing on their pinky-blue palms
trays of Britannia metal with tall glasses and fresh
bunches of mint, shouting orders to dozing menials,
and calling to each other from opposite ends of
the court; and finally the stoutest of the three,
disappearing from view, reappeared suddenly on
a pale green balcony overhead, where, profiled
against a square of blue sky, she leaned over in a
Veronese attitude and screamed down to the others
like an excited parrot.

In spite of their febrile activity and tropical
bird-shrieks, we waited in vain for tea; and after

a while our host suggested to his son that I might like to visit the ladies of the household. As I had expected, the young man led me across the *patio*, lifted the cotton hanging and introduced me into an apartment exactly like the one we had just left. Divans covered with striped mattress-ticking stood against the white walls, and on them sat seven or eight passive-looking women over whom a number of pale children scrambled.

The eldest of the group, and evidently the mistress of the house, was an Algerian lady, probably of about fifty, with a sad and delicately-modelled face; the others were daughters, daughters-in-law and concubines. The latter word evokes to occidental ears images of sensual seduction which the Moroccan harem seldom realizes. All the ladies of this dignified official household wore the same look of somewhat melancholy respectability. In their stuffy curtained apartment they were like cellar-grown flowers, pale, heavy, fuller but frailer than the garden sort. Their dresses, rich but sober, the veils and diadems put on in honour of my visit, had a dignified dowdiness in odd contrast to the frivolity of the Imperial harem. But what chiefly struck me was the apathy of the younger women. I asked them if they had a garden, and they shook their heads wistfully, saying that there were no gardens in Old Fez. The roof was therefore their only escape: a roof overlooking acres and acres of other roofs, and closed in by the naked fortified mountains which stand about Fez like prison-walls.

After a brief exchange of compliments silence fell. Conversing through interpreters is a benumbing process, and there are few points of contact between the open-air occidental mind and beings imprisoned in a conception of sexual and domestic life based on slave-service and incessant espionage. These languid women on their muslin cushions toil not, neither do they spin. The Moroccan lady knows little of cooking, needlework or any household arts. When her child is ill she can only hang it with amulets and wail over it; the great lady of the Fazi palace is as ignorant of hygiene as the peasant-woman of the *bled*. And all these colourless eventless lives depend on the favour of one fat tyrannical man, bloated with good living and authority, himself almost as inert and sedentary as his women, and accustomed to impose his whims on them ever since he ran about the same *patio* as a little short-smocked boy.

The redeeming point in this stagnant domesticity is the tenderness of the parents for their children, and western writers have laid so much stress on this that one would suppose children could be loved only by inert and ignorant parents. It is in fact charming to see the heavy eyes of the Moroccan father light up when a brown grass-hopper baby jumps on his knee, and the unfeigned tenderness with which the childless women of the harem caress the babies of their happier rivals. But the sentimentalist moved by this display of family feeling would do well to consider the lives of these much-petted children. Ignorance, unhealthiness and a precocious sexual initiation prevail in all classes. Education consists in learning by heart endless passages of the Koran, and amusement in assisting at spectacles that would be unintelligible to western children, but that the pleasantries of the harem make perfectly comprehensible to Moroccan infancy. At eight or nine the little girls are married, at twelve the son of the house is "given his first negress"; and thereafter, in the rich and leisured

From a photograph from "France-Maroc"

Women watching a procession from a roof

class, both sexes live till old age in an atmosphere of sensuality without seduction.

The young son of the house led me back across the court, where the negresses were still shrieking and scurrying, and passing to and fro like a stage-procession with the vain paraphernalia of a tea that never came. Our host still smiled from his cushions, resigned to Oriental delays. To distract the impatient westerners, a servant unhooked from the wall the cage of a gently-cooing dove. It was brought to us, still cooing, and looked at me with the same resigned and vacant eyes as the ladies I had just left. As it was being restored to its hook the slaves lolling about the entrance scattered respectfully at the approach of a handsome man of about thirty, with delicate features and a black beard. Crossing the court, he stooped to kiss the shoulder of our host, who introduced him as his eldest son, the husband of one or two of the little pale wives with whom I had been exchanging platitudes.

From the increasing agitation of the negresses it became evident that the ceremony of tea-making had been postponed till his arrival. A metal tray bearing a Britannia samovar and tea-pot was placed on the tiles of the court, and squatting beside it the newcomer gravely proceeded to infuse the mint. Suddenly the cotton hangings fluttered again, and a tiny child in the scantest of smocks rushed out and scampered across the court. Our venerable host, stretching out rapturous arms, caught the fugitive to his bosom, where the little boy lay like a squirrel, watching us with great sidelong eyes. He was the last-born of the patriarch, and the youngest brother of the majestic bearded gentleman engaged in tea-making. While he was still in his father's arms two more sons appeared: charming almond-eyed schoolboys returning from their Koran-class, escorted by their slaves. All the sons greeted each other affectionately, and caressed with almost feminine tenderness the dancing baby so lately added to their ranks; and finally, to crown this scene of domestic intimacy, the three negresses, their gigantic effort at last accomplished, passed about glasses of steaming mint and trays of gazelles' horns and white sugar-cakes.

VI

IN MARRAKECH

THE farther one travels from the Mediterranean
and Europe the closer the curtains of the women's
quarters are drawn. The only harem in which
we were allowed an interpreter was that of the
Sultan himself; in the private harems of Fez and
Rabat a French-speaking relative transmitted (or
professed to transmit) our remarks; in Marrakech,
the great nobleman and dignitary who kindly invited me to visit his household was deaf to our
hint that the presence of a lady from one of the
French government schools might facilitate our
intercourse.

When we drove up to his palace, one of the
stateliest in Marrakech, the street was thronged
with clansmen and clients. Dignified merchants
in white muslin, whose grooms held white mules
saddled with rose-coloured velvet, warriors from
the Atlas wearing the corkscrew ringlets which
are a sign of military prowess, Jewish traders in
black gabardines, leather-gaitered peasant-women
with chickens and cheese, and beggars rolling their

[197]

blind eyes or exposing their fly-plastered sores, were gathered in Oriental promiscuity about the great man's door; while under the archway stood a group of youths and warlike-looking older men who were evidently of his own clan.

The Caïd's chamberlain, a middle-aged man of dignified appearance, advanced to meet us between bowing clients and tradesmen. He led us through cool passages lined with the intricate mosaic-work of Fez, past beggars who sat on stone benches whining out their blessings, and pale Fazi craftsmen laying a floor of delicate tiles. The Caïd is a lover of old Arab architecture. His splendid house, which is not yet finished, has been planned and decorated on the lines of the old Imperial palaces, and when a few years of sun and rain and Oriental neglect have worked their way on its cedar-wood and gilding and ivory stucco it will have the same faded loveliness as the fairy palaces of Fez.

In a garden where fountains splashed and roses climbed among cypresses, the Caïd himself awaited us. This great fighter and loyal friend of France is a magnificent eagle-beaked man, brown, lean and sinewy, with vigilant eyes looking out under his carefully draped muslin turban, and negroid lips half-hidden by a close black beard.

Tea was prepared in the familiar setting; a long arcaded room with painted ceiling and richly stuccoed walls. All around were ranged the usual mattresses covered with striped ticking and piled with muslin cushions. A bedstead of brass, imitating a Louis XVI cane bed, and adorned with brass garlands and bows, throned on the usual platform; and the only other ornaments were a few clocks and bunches of wax flowers under glass. Like all Orientals, this hero of the Atlas, who spends half his life with his fighting clansmen in a mediæval stronghold among the snows, and the other half rolling in a 60 h.p. motor over smooth French roads, seems unaware of any degrees of beauty or appropriateness in objects of European design, and places against the exquisite mosaics and traceries of his Fazi craftsmen the tawdriest bric-à-brac of the cheap department-store.

While tea was being served I noticed a tiny negress, not more than six or seven years old, who stood motionless in the embrasure of an archway. Like most of the Moroccan slaves, even in the greatest households, she was shabbily, almost raggedly, dressed. A dirty *gandourah* of striped muslin covered her faded caftan, and a cheap kerchief was wound above her grave and precocious little face. With preternatural vigilance she watched each movement of the Caïd, who never spoke to her, looked at her, or made her the slightest perceptible sign, but whose least wish she instantly divined, refilling his tea-cup, passing the plates of sweets, or removing our empty glasses, in obedience to some secret telegraphy on which her whole being hung.

The Caïd is a great man. He and his famous elder brother, holding the southern marches of Morocco against alien enemies and internal rebellion, played a preponderant part in the defence of the French colonies in North Africa during the long struggle of the war. Enlightened, cultivated, a friend of the arts, a scholar and diplomatist, he seems, unlike many Orientals, to have selected the best in assimilating European influences. Yet when I looked at the tiny creature watching him with those anxious joyless eyes I felt once more the abyss that slavery and the seraglio put between the most Europeanized Mahometan and the western conception of life. The Caïd's little black slaves are well-known in Morocco, and behind the sad child leaning in the archway stood all the shadowy evils of the social system that hangs like a millstone about the neck of Islam.

Presently a handsome tattered negress came across the garden to invite me to the harem. Captain de S. and his wife, who had accompanied me, were old friends of the Chief's, and it was owing to this that the jealously-guarded doors of the women's quarters were opened to Mme de S. and myself. We followed the negress to a marble-paved court where pigeons fluttered and strutted about the central fountain. From under a trellised arcade hung with linen curtains several ladies came forward. They greeted my companion with exclamations of delight; then they led us into the usual commonplace room with divans and white-washed walls. Even in the most sumptuous Moroccan palaces little care seems to be expended on the fittings of the women's quarters: unless, indeed, the room in which visitors are received corresponds with a boarding-school "parlour," and

the personal touch is reserved for the private apartments.

The ladies who greeted us were more richly
dressed than any I had seen except the Sultan's
favourites; but their faces were more distinguished,
more European in outline, than those of the round-
cheeked beauties of Rabat. My companions had
told me that the Caïd's harem was recruited from
Georgia, and that the ladies receiving us had been
brought up in the relative freedom of life in Constantinople; and it was easy to read in their wistfully smiling eyes memories of a life unknown to
the passive daughters of Morocco.

They appeared to make no secret of their regrets,
for presently one of them, with a smile, called my
attention to some faded photographs hanging over
the divan. They represented groups of plump pro-
vincial-looking young women in dowdy European
ball-dresses; and it required an effort of the imagination to believe that the lovely creatures in velvet
caftans, with delicately tattooed temples under complicated head-dresses, and hennaed feet crossed on
muslin cushions, were the same as the beaming
frumps in the photographs. But to the sump-

tuously-clad exiles these faded photographs and ugly dresses represented freedom, happiness, and all they had forfeited when fate (probably in the shape of an opulent Hebrew couple "travelling with their daughters") carried them from the Bosphorus to the Atlas.

As in the other harems I had visited, perfect equality seemed to prevail between the ladies, and while they chatted with Mme de S. whose few words of Arabic had loosed their tongues, I tried to guess which was the favourite, or at least the first in rank. My choice wavered between the pretty pale creature with a *ferronnière* across her temples and a tea-rose caftan veiled in blue gauze, and the nut-brown beauty in red velvet hung with pearls whose languid attitudes and long-lidded eyes were so like the Keepsake portraits of Byron's Haïdee. Or was it perhaps the third, less pretty but more vivid and animated, who sat behind the tea-tray, and mimicked so expressively a soldier shouldering his rifle, and another falling dead, in her effort to ask us "when the dreadful war would be over"? Perhaps . . . unless, indeed, it were the handsome octoroon, slightly older than the others, but even more richly dressed, so free and noble in her movements, and treated by the others with such friendly deference.

I was struck by the fact that among them all there was not a child; it was the first harem without babies that I had seen in that prolific land. Presently one of the ladies asked Mme. de S. about her children; in reply, she enquired for the Caïd's little boy, the son of his wife who had died. The ladies' faces lit up wistfully, a slave was given an order, and presently a large-eyed ghost of a child was brought into the room.

Instantly all the bracelet-laden arms were held out to the dead woman's son; and as I watched the weak little body hung with amulets and the heavy head covered with thin curls pressed against a brocaded bosom, I was reminded of one of the coral-hung child-Christs of Crivelli, standing livid and waxen on the knee of a splendidly dressed Madonna.

The poor baby on whom such hopes and ambitions hung stared at us with a solemn unamused gaze. Would all his pretty mothers, his eyes seemed to ask, succeed in bringing him to maturity in spite of the parched summers of the south and the stifling existence of the harem? It was evident that no precaution had been neglected to protect him from maleficent influences and the danger that walks by night, for his frail neck and wrists were hung with innumerable charms: Koranic verses, Soudanese incantations, and images of forgotten idols in amber and coral and horn and ambergris. Perhaps they will ward off the powers of evil, and let him grow up to shoulder the burden of the great Caïds of the south.

VI

GENERAL LYAUTEY'S WORK IN MOROCCO

VI

GENERAL LYAUTEY'S WORK IN MOROCCO

I

IT is not too much to say that General Lyautey has twice saved Morocco from destruction: once in 1912, when the inertia and double-dealing of Abd-el-Hafid abandoned the country to the rebellious tribes who had attacked him in Fez, and the second time in August, 1914, when Germany declared war on France.

In 1912, in consequence of the threatening attitude of the dissident tribes and the generally disturbed condition of the country, the Sultan Abd-el-Hafid had asked France to establish a protectorate in Morocco. The agreement entered into, called the "Convention of Fez," stipulated that a French Resident-General should be sent to Morocco with authority to act as the Sultan's sole representative in treating with the other powers. The convention was signed in March, 1912, and a few days afterward an uprising more serious than any that had gone before took place in Fez. This sudden outbreak was due in part to purely local and native difficulties, in part to the intrinsic weakness of the French situation. The French government had imagined that a native army commanded by French officers could be counted on to support the Makhzen and maintain order; but Abd-el-Hafid's growing unpopularity had estranged his own people from him, and the army turned on the government and on the French. On the 17th of April, 1912, the Moroccan soldiers massacred their French officers after inflicting horrible tortures on them; the population of Fez rose against the European civilians, and for a fortnight the Oued Fez ran red with the blood of harmless French colonists. It was then that France appointed General Lyautey Resident-General in Morocco.

When he reached Fez it was besieged by twenty thousand Berbers. Rebel tribes were flocking in to their support, to the cry of the Holy War; and the terrified Sultan, who had already announced his intention of resigning, warned the French troops who were trying to protect him that unless they guaranteed to get him safely to Rabat he would turn his influence against them. Two days afterward the Berbers attacked Fez and broke in at two gates. The French drove them out and forced them back twenty miles. The outskirts of the city were rapidly fortified, and a few weeks later General Gouraud, attacking the rebels in the valley of the Sebou, completely disengaged Fez.

The military danger overcome, General Lyautey began his great task of civilian administration. His aim was to support and strengthen the existing government, to reassure and pacify the distrustful and antagonistic elements, and to assert French authority without irritating or discouraging native ambitions.

Meanwhile a new Mahdi (Anmed-el-Hiba) had risen in the south. Treacherously supported by Abd-el-Hafid, he was proclaimed Sultan at Tiznit, and acknowledged by the whole of the Souss. In Marrakech, native unrest had caused the Europeans to fly to the coast, and in the north a new group of rebellious tribes menaced Fez.

El-Hiba entered Marrakech in August, 1912, and

the French consul and several other French residents were taken prisoner. El-Hiba's forces then advanced to a point half way between Marrakech and Mazagan, where General Mangin, at that time a colonial colonel, met and utterly routed them. The disorder in the south, and the appeals of the native population for protection against the savage depredations of the new Mahdist rebels, made it necessary for the French troops to follow up their success; and in September Marrakech was taken.

Such were the swift and brilliant results of General Lyautey's intervention. The first difficulties had been quickly overcome; others, far more complicated, remained. The military occupation of Morocco had to be followed up by its civil reorganization. By the Franco-German treaty of 1911 Germany had finally agreed to recognize the French protectorate in Morocco; but in spite of an apparently explicit acknowledgment of this right, Germany, as usual, managed to slip into the contract certain ambiguities of form that were likely to lead to future trouble.

To obtain even this incomplete treaty France had had to sacrifice part of her colonies in equatorial Africa; and in addition to the uncertain relation with Germany there remained the dead weight of the Spanish zone and the confused international administration of Tangier. The disastrously misgoverned Spanish zone has always been a centre for German intrigue and native conspiracies, as well as a permanent obstacle to the economic development of Morocco.

Such were the problems that General Lyautey found awaiting him. A long colonial experience, and an unusual combination of military and administrative talents, prepared him for the almost impossible task of dealing with them. Swift and decisive when military action is required, he has above all the long views and endless patience necessary to the successful colonial governor. The policy of France in Morocco has been weak and spasmodic; in his hands it became firm and consecutive. A sympathetic understanding of the native prejudices, and a real affection for the native character, made him try to build up an administration which should be, not an application of French ideas to African conditions, but a development of the best native aspirations. The difficulties were immense. The attempt to govern as far as possible through the Great Chiefs was a wise one; but it was hampered by the fact that these powerful leaders, however loyal to the Protectorate, knew no methods of administration but those based on extortion. It was necessary at once to use them and to educate them; and one of General Lyautey's greatest achievements has been the successful employment of native ability in the government of the country.

II

THE first thing to do was to create a strong frontier against the dissident tribes of the Blad-es-Siba. To do this it was necessary that the French should hold the natural defenses of the country, the foothills of the Little and of the Great Atlas, and the valley of the Moulouya, which forms the corridor between western Algeria and Morocco. This was nearly accomplished in 1914 when war broke out.

At that moment the home government cabled the Resident-General to send all his available troops to France, abandoning the whole of conquered territory except the coast towns. To do so would have been to give France's richest colonies*

* The loss of Morocco would inevitably have been followed by that of the whole of French North Africa.

outright to Germany at a moment when what they could supply—meat and wheat—was exactly what the enemy most needed.

General Lyautey took forty-eight hours to consider. He then decided to "empty the egg without breaking the shell"; and the reply he sent was that of a great patriot and a great general. In effect he said: "I will give you all the troops you ask, but instead of abandoning the interior of the country I will hold what we have already taken, and fortify and enlarge our boundaries." No other military document has so nearly that ring as Marshal Foch's immortal Marne despatch (written only a few weeks later): "My centre is broken, my right wing is wavering, the situation is favorable and I am about to attack."

General Lyautey had framed his answer in a moment of patriotic exaltation, when the soul of every Frenchman was strung up to a superhuman pitch. But the pledge once made, it had to be carried out; and even those who most applauded his decision wondered how he would meet the almost insuperable difficulties it involved. Morocco, when he was called there, was already honeycombed by German trading interests and secret political intrigue, and the fruit seemed ready to fall when the declaration of war shook the bough. The only way to save the colony for France was to keep its industrial and agricultural life going, and give to the famous "business as usual" a really justifiable application.

General Lyautey completely succeeded, and the first impression of all travellers arriving in Morocco two years later was that of suddenly returning to a world in normal conditions. There was even, so complete was the illusion, a first moment of almost painful surprise on entering an active prosperous community, seemingly absorbed in immediate material interests to the exclusion of all thought of the awful drama that was being played out in the mother country; and it was only on reflection that this absorption in the day's task, and this air of smiling faith in the future, were seen to be Morocco's truest way of serving France.

For not only was France to be supplied with provisions, but the confidence in her ultimate triumph was at all costs to be kept up in the native mind. German influence was as deep-seated as a

cancer: to cut it out required the most drastic of
operations. And that operation consisted precisely
in letting it be seen that France was strong and
prosperous enough for her colonies to thrive and
expand without fear while she held at bay on her
own frontier the most formidable foe the world has
ever seen. Such was the "policy of the smile,"
consistently advocated by General Lyautey from
the beginning of the war, and of which he and his
household were the first to set the example.

III

THE General had said that he would not "break
the egg-shell"; but he knew that this was not
enough, and that he must make it appear unbreak-
able if he were to retain the confidence of the
natives.

How this was achieved, with the aid of the few
covering troops left him, is still almost incomprehensible. To hold the line was virtually impossible: therefore he pushed it forward. An anony-
mous writer in *L'Afrique Française* (January, 1917)
has thus described the manœuvre: "General Henrys
was instructed to watch for storm-signals on the

front, to stop up the cracks, to strengthen weak points and to rectify doubtful lines. Thanks to these operations, which kept the rebels perpetually harassed by always forestalling their own plans, the occupied territory was enlarged by a succession of strongly fortified positions." While this was going on in the north, General Lamothe was extending and strengthening, by means of pacific negotiations, the influence of the Great Chiefs in the south; and other agents of the Residency were engaged in watching and thwarting the incessant German intrigues in the Spanish zone.

General Lyautey is quoted as having said that "a work-shop is worth a battalion." This precept he managed to put into action even during the first dark days of 1914, and the interior development of Morocco proceeded side by side with the strengthening of its defenses. Germany had long foreseen what an asset northwest Africa would be during the war; and General Lyautey was determined to prove how right Germany had been. He did so by getting the government, to whom he had given nearly all his troops, to give him in exchange an agricultural and industrial army, or at least enough specialists to form such an army out of the available material in the country. For every battle fought a road was made;* for every rebel fortress shelled a factory was built, a harbor developed, or more miles of fallow land ploughed and sown.

But this economic development did not satisfy the Resident. He wished Morocco to enlarge her commercial relations with France and the other allied countries, and with this object in view he organized and carried out with brilliant success a series of exhibitions at Casablanca, Fez and Rabat. The result of this bold policy surpassed even its creator's hopes. The Moroccans of the plain are an industrious and money-loving people, and the sight of these rapidly improvised exhibitions, where the industrial and artistic products of France and other European countries were shown in picturesque buildings grouped about flower-filled gardens, fascinated their imagination and strengthened their confidence in the country that could find time for

---

* During the first year of the war roads were built in Morocco by German prisoners; and it was because Germany was so thoroughly aware of the economic value of the country, and so anxious not to have her prestige diminished, that she immediately protested, on the absurd plea of the unwholesomeness of the climate, and threatened reprisals unless the prisoners were withdrawn.

[219]

such an effort in the midst of a great war. The Voice of the Bazaar carried the report to the farthest confines of Moghreb, and one by one the notabilities of the different tribes arrived, with delegations from Algeria and Tunisia. It was even said that several rebel chiefs had submitted to the Makhzen in order not to miss the Exhibition.

At the same time as the "Miracle of the Marne" another, less famous but almost as vital to France, was being silently performed at the other end of her dominions. It will not seem an exaggeration to speak of General Lyautey's achievement during the first year of the war as the "Miracle of Morocco" if one considers the immense importance of doing what he did at the moment when he did it. And to understand this it is only needful to reckon what Germany could have drawn in supplies and men from a German North Africa, and what would have been the situation of France during the war with a powerful German colony in control of the western Mediterranean.

General Lyautey has always been one of the clear-sighted administrators who understand that the successful government of a foreign country depends on many little things, and not least on the administrator's genuine sympathy with the traditions, habits and tastes of the people. A keen feeling for beauty had prepared him to appreciate all that was most exquisite and venerable in the Arab art of Morocco, and even in the first struggle with political and military problems he found time to gather about him a group of archœologists and artists who were charged with the inspection and preservation of the national monuments and the revival of the languishing native art-industries. The old pottery, jewelry, metal-work, rugs and embroideries of the different regions were carefully collected and classified; schools of decorative art were founded, skilled artisans sought out, and every effort was made to urge European residents to follow native models and use native artisans in building and furnishing.

At the various Exhibitions much space was allotted to these revived industries, and the matting of Salé, the rugs of Rabat, the embroideries of Fez and Marrakech have already found a ready market in France, besides awakening in the educated class of colonists an appreciation of the old buildings and the old arts of the country that will be its surest safeguard against the destructive effects of colonial expansion. It is only necessary to see the havoc wrought in Tunisia and Algeria by the heavy hand of the colonial government to know what General Lyautey has achieved in saving Morocco from this form of destruction, also.

All this has been accomplished by the Resident-General during five years of unexampled and incessant difficulty; and probably the true explanation of the miracle is that which he himself gives when he says, with the quiet smile that typifies his Moroccan war-policy: "It was easy to do because I loved the people."

THE WORK OF THE FRENCH PROTECTORATE, 1912–1918

PORTS

Owing to the fact that the neglected and roadless Spanish zone intervened between the French possessions and Tangier, which is the natural port of Morocco, one of the first pre-occupations of General Lyautey was to make ports along the inhospitable Atlantic coast, where there are no natural harbours.

Since 1912, in spite of the immense cost and the difficulty of obtaining labour, the following has been done:

Casablanca. A jetty 1900 metres long has been planned: 824 metres finished December, 1917.

Small jetty begun 1916, finished 1917: length 330 metres. Small harbour thus created shelters small boats (150 tons) in all weathers.

Quays 747 metres long already finished.

16 steam-cranes working.

Warehouses and depots covering 41,985 square metres completed.

Rabat. Work completed December, 1917.

A quay 200 metres long, to which boats with a draught of three metres can tie up.

Two groups of warehouses, steam-cranes, etc., covering 22,600 square metres.

A quay 100 metres long on the Salé side of the river.

Kenitra. The port of Kenitra is at the mouth of the Sebou River, and is capable of becoming a good river port.

The work up to December, 1917, comprises:

A channel 100 metres long and three metres deep, cut through the bar of the Sebou.

Jetties built on each side of the channel.

Quay 100 metres long.

Building of sheds, depots, warehouses, steam-cranes, etc.

At the ports of Fedalah, Mazagan, Safi, Mogador and Agadir similar plans are in course of execution.

COMMERCE

COMPARATIVE TABLES

1912	1918
Total Commerce	Total Commerce
Fcs. 177,737,723	Fcs. 386,238,618
Exports	Exports
Fcs. 67,080,383	Fcs. 116,148,081

GENERAL LYAUTEY'S WORK IN MOROCCO

ROADS BUILT
National roads . . . . 2,074 kilometres
Secondary roads . . . . 569 "

RAILWAYS BUILT
622 kilometres

LAND CULTIVATED

1915	1918
Approximate area	Approximate area
21,165.17 hectares	1,681,308.03 hectares

JUSTICE

1. Creation of French courts for French nationals and those under French protection. These take cognizance of civil cases where both parties, or even one, are amenable to French jurisdiction.

2. Moroccan law is Moslem, and administered by Moslem magistrates. Private law, including that of inheritance, is based on the Koran. The Sultan has maintained the principle whereby real property and administrative cases fall under native law. These courts are as far as possible supervised and controlled by the establishment of a Cherifian Ministry of Justice to which the native Judges are responsible. Special care is taken to prevent the alienation of property held collectively, or any similar transactions likely to produce political and economic disturbances.

3. Criminal jurisdiction is delegated to Pashas and Cadis by the Sultan, except of offenses committed against, or in conjunction with, French nationals and those under French protection. Such cases come before the tribunals of the French Protectorate.

[224]

GENERAL LYAUTEY'S WORK IN MOROCCO

EDUCATION

The object of the Protectorate has been, on the one hand, to give to the children of French colonists in Morocco the same education as they would have received at elementary and secondary schools in France; on the other, to provide the indigenous population with a system of education that shall give to the young Moroccans an adequate commercial or manual training, or prepare them for administrative posts, but without interfering with their native customs or beliefs.

Before 1912 there existed in Morocco only a few small schools supported by the French Legation at Tangier and by the Alliance Française, and a group of Hebrew schools in the Mellahs, maintained by the Universal Israelite Alliance.

1912.	Total number of schools	37
1918.	" " " "	191
1912.	Total number of pupils	3006
1918.	" " " "	21,520
1912.	Total number of teachers	61
1918.	" " " "	668

In addition to the French and indigenous schools, sewing-schools have been formed for the native girls and have been exceptionally successful.

Moslem colleges have been founded at Rabat and Fez in order to supplement the native education of young Mahometans of the upper classes, who intend to take up wholesale business or banking, or prepare for political, judicial or administrative posts under the Sultan's government. The course lasts four years and comprises: Arabic, French, mathematics, history, geography, religious (Mahometan) instruction, and the law of the Koran.

The "Ecole Supérieure de la langue arabe et des dialectes berbères" at Rabat receives European and Moroccan students. The courses are: Arabic, the Berber dialects, Arab literature, ethnography, administrative Moroccan law, Moslem law, Berber customary law.

MEDICAL AID

The Protectorate has established 113 medical centres for the native population, ranging from simple dispensaries and small native infirmaries to the important hospitals of Rabat, Fez, Meknez, Marrakech, and Casablanca

Mobile sanitary formations supplied with light motor ambulances travel about the country, vaccinating, making tours of sanitary inspection, investigating infected areas, and giving general hygienic education throughout the remoter regions.

Native patients treated in 1916 . . . . . over 900,000
" " " " 1917 . . . . . " 1,220,800

Night-shelters in towns. Every town is provided with a shelter for the indigent wayfarers so numerous in Morocco. These shelters are used as disinfection centres, from which suspicious cases are sent to quarantine camp at the gates of the towns.

Central Laboratory at Rabat. This is a kind of Pasteur Institute. In 1917, 210,000 persons were vaccinated throughout the country and 356 patients treated at the Laboratory for rabies.

Clinics for venereal diseases have been established at Casablanca, Fez, Rabat, and Marrakech.

More than 15,000 cases were treated in 1917.

Ophthalmic clinics in the same cities gave in 1917, 44,600 consultations.

Radiotherapy. Clinics have been opened at Fez and Rabat for the treatment of skin diseases of the head, from which the native children habitually suffer.

The French Department of Health distributes annually immense quantities of quinine in the malarial districts.

Madame Lyautey's private charities comprise admirably administered child-welfare centres in the principal cities, with dispensaries for the native mothers and children.

VII

A SKETCH OF MOROCCAN HISTORY

VII

A SKETCH OF MOROCCAN HISTORY

I

THE BERBERS

IN the briefest survey of the Moroccan past account must first of all be taken of the factor which, from the beginning of recorded events, has conditioned the whole history of North Africa: the existence, from the Sahara to the Mediterranean, of a mysterious irreducible indigenous race with which every successive foreign rule, from Carthage to France, has had to reckon, and which has

NOTE.—In the chapters on Moroccan history and art I have tried to set down a slight and superficial outline of a large and confused subject. In extenuation of this summary attempt I hasten to explain that its chief merit is its lack of originality.

Its facts are chiefly drawn from the books mentioned in the short bibliography at the end of the volume; in addition to which I am deeply indebted for information given on the spot to the group of remarkable specialists attached to the French administration, and to the cultivated and cordial French officials, military and civilian, who, at each stage of my rapid journey, did their best to answer my questions and open my eyes.

but imperfectly and partially assimilated the language, the religion, and the culture that successive civilizations have tried to impose upon it.

This race, the race of Berbers, has never, modern explorers tell us, become really Islamite, any more than it ever really became Phenician, Roman or Vandal. It has imposed its habits while it appeared to adopt those of its invaders, and has perpetually represented, outside the Ismalitic and Hispano-Arabic circle of the Makhzen, the vast tormenting element of the dissident, the rebellious, the unsubdued tribes of the Blad-es-Siba.

Who were these indigenous tribes with whom the Phenicians, when they founded their first counting-houses on the north and west coast of Africa, exchanged stuffs and pottery and arms for ivory, ostrich-feathers and slaves?

Historians frankly say they do not know. All sorts of material obstacles have hitherto hampered the study of Berber origins; but it seems clear that from the earliest historic times they were a mixed race, and the ethnologist who attempts to define them is faced by the same problem as the historian of modern America who should try to find the racial definition of an "American." For centuries, for ages, North Africa has been what America now is: the clearing-house of the world. When at length it occurred to the explorer that the natives of North Africa were not all Arabs or Moors, he was bewildered by the many vistas of all they were or might be: so many and tangled were the threads leading up to them, so interwoven was their pre-Islamite culture with worn-out shreds of older and richer societies.

M. Saladin, in his "Manuel d'Architecture Musulmane," after attempting to unravel the influences which went to the making of the mosque of Kairouan, the walls of Marrakech, the Medersas of Fez—influences that lead him back to Chaldæan branch-huts, to the walls of Babylon and the embroideries of Coptic Egypt—somewhat despairingly sums up the result: "The principal elements contributed to Moslem art by the styles preceding it may be thus enumerated: from India, floral ornament; from Persia, the structural principles of the Acheminedes, and the Sassanian vault. Mesopotamia contributes a system of vaulting, incised ornament, and proportion; the Copts, ornamental detail in general; Egypt, mass and unbroken wall-spaces; Spain, construction and Romano-Iberian ornament; Africa, decorative detail and Romano-Berber traditions (with Byzantine influences in Persia); Asia Minor, a mixture of Byzantine and Persian characteristics."

As with the art of North Africa, so with its supposedly indigenous population. The Berber dialects extend from the Lybian desert to Senegal. Their language was probably related to Coptic, itself related to the ancient Egyptian and the non-Semitic dialects of Abyssinia and Nubia. Yet philologists have discovered what appears to be a far-off link between the Berber and Semitic languages, and the Chleuhs of the Draa and the Souss, with their tall slim Egyptian-looking bodies and hooked noses, may have a strain of Semitic blood. M. Augustin Bernard, in speaking of the natives of North Africa, ends, much on the same note as M. Saladin in speaking of Moslem art: "In their blood are the sediments of many races, Phenician, Punic, Egyptian and Arab."

They were not, like the Arabs, wholly nomadic; but the tent, the flock, the tribe always entered into their conception of life. M. Augustin Bernard has pointed out that, in North Africa, the sedentary and nomadic habit do not imply a permanent difference, but rather a temporary one of situation and opportunity. The sedentary Berbers are nomadic in certain conditions; and from the earliest times the invading nomad Berbers tended to become sedentary when they reached the rich plains north of the Atlas. But when they built cities it was as their ancestors and their neighbours pitched tents; and they destroyed or abandoned them as lightly as their desert forbears packed their camelbags and moved to new pastures. Everywhere behind the bristling walls and rock-clamped towers of old Morocco lurks the shadowy spirit of instability. Every new Sultan builds himself a new house and lets his predecessors' palaces fall into decay; and as with the Sultan so with his vassals and officials. Change is the rule in this apparently unchanged civilization, where "nought may abide but Mutability."

II

PHENICIANS, ROMANS AND VANDALS

FAR to the south of the Anti-Atlas, in the yellow deserts that lead to Timbuctoo, live the wild Touaregs, the Veiled Men of the south, who ride to war with their faces covered by linen masks.

These Veiled Men are Berbers; but their alphabet is composed of Lybian characters, and these are closely related to the signs engraved on certain vases of the Nile valley that are probably six thousand years old. Moreover, among the rock-cut images of the African desert is the likeness of Theban Ammon crowned with the solar disk between serpents; and the old Berber religion, with its sun and animal worship, has many points of resemblance with Egyptian beliefs. All this implies trade contacts far below the horizon of history, and obscure comings and goings of restless throngs across incredible distances long before the Phenicians planted their first trading posts on the north African coast about 1200 B. C.

Five hundred years before Christ, Carthage sent one of her admirals on a voyage of colonization

beyond the Pillars of Hercules. Hannon set out
with sixty fifty-oared galleys carrying thirty thousand people. Some of them settled at Mehedyia,
at the mouth of the Sebou, where Phenician remains
have been found; and apparently the exploration
was pushed as far south as the coast of Guinea, for
the inscription recording it relates that Hannon beheld elephants, hairy men and "savages called
gorillas." At any rate, Carthage founded stable
colonies at Melilla, Larache, Salé and Casablanca.

Then came the Romans, who carried on the
business, set up one of their easy tolerant protecto-
rates over "Tingitanian Mauretania," * and built
one important military outpost, Volubilis in the
Zerhoun, which a series of minor defenses probably
connected with Salé on the west coast, thus guarding the Roman province against the unconquered
Berbers to the south.

Tingitanian Mauretania was one of the numerous
African granaries of Rome. She also supplied the
Imperial armies with their famous African cavalry;
and among minor articles of exportation were

* East of the Moulouya, the African protectorate (now west Algeria and
the Sud Oranais) was called the Mauretania of Cæsar.

guinea-hens, snails, honey, euphorbia, wild beasts,
horses and pearls. The Roman dominion ceased
at the line drawn between Volubilis and Salé.
There was no interest in pushing farther south,
since the ivory and slave trade with the Soudan
was carried on by way of Tripoli. But the spirit of
enterprise never slept in the race, and Pliny records
the journey of a Roman general—Suetonius Pau-
linus—who appears to have crossed the Atlas, probably by the pass of Tizi-n-Telremt, which is even
now so beset with difficulties that access by land
to the Souss will remain an arduous undertaking
until the way by Imintanout is safe for European
travel.

The Vandals swept away the Romans in the fifth
century. The Lower Empire restored a brief period
of civilization; but its authority finally dwindled to
the half-legendary rule of Count Julian, shut up
within his walls of Ceuta. Then Europe vanished
from the shores of Africa; and though Christianity
lingered here and there in vague Donatist colonies,
and in the names of Roman bishoprics, its last
faint hold went down in the eighth century before
the irresistible cry: "There is no God but Allah!"

A SKETCH OF MOROCCAN HISTORY

III

THE ARAB CONQUEST

THE first Arab invasion of Morocco is said to have reached the Atlantic coast; but it left no lasting traces, and the real Islamisation of Barbary did not happen till near the end of the eighth century, when a descendant of Ali, driven from Mesopotamia by the Caliphate, reached the mountains above Volubilis and there founded an empire. The Berbers, though indifferent in religious matters, had always, from a spirit of independence, tended to heresy and schism. Under the rule of Christian Rome they had been Donatists, as M. Bernard puts it, "out of opposition to the Empire"; and so, out of opposition to the Caliphate, they took up the cause of one Moslem schismatic after another. Their great popular movements have always had a religious basis, or perhaps it would be truer to say, a religious pretext; for they have been in reality the partly moral, partly envious revolt of hungry and ascetic warrior tribes against the fatness and corruption of the "cities of the plain."

Idriss I became the first national saint and ruler

of Morocco. His rule extended throughout northern Morocco, and his son, Idriss II, attacking a
Berber tribe on the banks of the Oued Fez, routed
them, took possession of their oasis and founded
the city of Fez. Thither came schismatic refugees
from Kairouan and Moors from Andalusia. The
Islamite Empire of Morocco was founded, and
Idriss II has become the legendary ancestor of all
its subsequent rulers.

The Idrissite rule is a welter of obscure struggles
between rapidly melting groups of adherents. Its
chief features are: the founding of Moulay Idriss
and Fez, and the building of the mosques of El
Andalous and Kairouiyin at Fez for the two groups
of refugees from Tunisia and Spain. Meanwhile
the Caliphate of Cordova had reached the height
of its power, while that of the Fatimites extended
from the Nile to western Morocco, and the little
Idrissite empire, pulverized under the weight of
these expanding powers, became once more a dust
of disintegrated tribes.

It was only in the eleventh century that the dust
again conglomerated. Two Arab tribes from the
desert of the Hedjaz, suddenly driven westward by

the Fatimites, entered Morocco, not with a small military expedition, as the Arabs had hitherto done, but with a horde of emigrants reckoned as high as 200,000 families; and this first colonizing expedition was doubtless succeeded by others.

To strengthen their hold in Morocco the Arab colonists embraced the dynastic feuds of the Berbers. They inaugurated a period of general havoc which destroyed what little prosperity had survived the break-up of the Idrissite rule, and many Berber tribes took refuge in the mountains; but others remained and were merged with the invaders, reforming into new tribes of mixed Berber and Arab blood. This invasion was almost purely destructive; it marks one of the most desolate periods in the progress of the "wasteful Empire" of Moghreb.

IV

ALMORAVIDS AND ALMOHADS

WHILE the Hilalian Arabs were conquering and destroying northern Morocco another but more fruitful invasion was upon her from the south. The Almoravids, one of the tribes of Veiled Men

of the south, driven by the usual mixture of religious zeal and lust of booty, set out to invade the
rich black kingdoms north of the Sahara. Thence
they crossed the Atlas under their great chief,
Youssef-ben-Tachfin, and founded the city of Marrakech in 1062. From Marrakech they advanced
on Idrissite Fez and the valley of the Moulouya.
Fez rose against her conquerors, and Youssef put
all the male inhabitants to death. By 1084 he was
master of Tangier and the Rif, and his rule stretched
as far west as Tlemcen, Oran and finally Algiers.

His ambition drove him across the straits to
Spain, where he conquered one Moslem prince after
another and wiped out the luxurious civilization of
Moorish Andalusia. In 1086, at Zallarca, Youssef
gave battle to Alphonso VI of Castile and Leon.
The Almoravid army was a strange rabble of Arabs,
Berbers, blacks, wild tribes of the Sahara and
Christian mercenaries. They conquered the Spanish forces, and Youssef left to his successors an
empire extending from the Ebro to Senegal and
from the Atlantic coast of Africa to the borders of
Tunisia. But the empire fell to pieces of its own
weight, leaving little record of its brief and stormy

existence. While Youssef was routing the forces of Christianity at Zallarca in Spain, another schismatic tribe of his own people was detaching Marrakech and the south from his rule.

The leader of the new invasion was a Mahdi, one of the numerous Saviours of the World who have carried death and destruction throughout Islam. His name was Ibn-Toumert, and he had travelled in Egypt, Syria and Spain, and made the pilgrimage to Mecca. Preaching the doctrine of a purified monotheism, he called his followers the Almohads or Unitarians, to distinguish them from the polytheistic Almoravids, whose heresies he denounced. He fortified the city of Tinmel in the Souss, and built there a mosque of which the ruins still exist. When he died, in 1128, he designated as his successor Abd-el-Moumen, the son of a potter, who had been his disciple.

Abd-el-Moumen carried on the campaign against the Almoravids. He fought them not only in Morocco but in Spain, taking Cadiz, Cordova, Granada as well as Tlemcen and Fez. In 1152 his African dominion reached from Tripoli to the Souss, and he had formed a disciplined army in which

Christian mercenaries from France and Spain
fought side by side with Berbers and Soudanese.
This great captain was also a great administrator,
and under his rule Africa was surveyed from the
Souss to Barka, the country was policed, agriculture
was protected, and the caravans journeyed safely
over the trade-routes.

Abd-el-Moumen died in 1163 and was followed
by his son, who, though he suffered reverses in
Spain, was also a great ruler. He died in 1184, and
his son, Yacoub-el-Mansour, avenged his father's
ill-success in Spain by the great victory of Alarcos
and the conquest of Madrid. Yacoub-el-Mansour
was the greatest of Moroccan Sultans. So far did
his fame extend that the illustrious Saladin sent
him presents and asked the help of his fleet. He
was a builder as well as a fighter, and the noblest
period of Arab art in Morocco and Spain coincides
with his reign.

After his death, the Almohad empire followed
the downward curve to which all Oriental rule
seems destined. In Spain, the Berber forces were
beaten in the great Christian victory of Las-Navas-
de Tolosa; and in Morocco itself the first stirrings

of the Beni-Merins (a new tribe from the Sahara) were preparing the way for a new dynasty.

V

THE MERINIDS

THE Beni-Merins or Merinids were nomads who ranged the desert between Biskra and the Tafilelt. It was not a religious upheaval that drove them to the conquest of Morocco. The demoralized Almohads called them in as mercenaries to defend their crumbling empire; and the Merinids came, drove out the Almohads, and replaced them.

They took Fez, Meknez, Salé, Rabat and Sidjilmassa in the Tafilelt; and their second Sultan, Abou-Youssef, built New Fez (Eldjid) on the height above the old Idrissite city. The Merinids renewed the struggle with the Sultan of Tlemcen, and carried the Holy War once more into Spain. The conflict with Tlemcen was long and unsuccessful, and one of the Merinid Sultans died assassinated under its walls. In the fourteenth century the Sultan Abou Hassan tried to piece together the scattered bits of the Almohad empire. Tlemcen was finally taken, and the whole of Algeria annexed. But in the plain of Kairouan, in Tunisia, Abou Hassan was defeated by the Arabs. Meanwhile one of his brothers had headed a revolt in Morocco, and the princes of Tlemcen won back their ancient kingdom. Constantine and Bougie rebelled in turn, and the kingdom of Abou Hassan vanished like a mirage. His successors struggled vainly to control their vassals in Morocco, and to keep their possessions beyond its borders. Before the end of the fourteenth century Morocco from end to end was a chaos of antagonistic tribes, owning no allegiance, abiding by no laws. The last of the Merinids, divided, diminished, bound by humiliating treaties with Christian Spain, kept up a semblance of sovereignty at Fez and Marrakech, at war with one another and with their neighbours; and Spain and Portugal seized this moment of internal dissolution to drive them from Spain, and carry the war into Morocco itself.

The short and stormy passage of the Beni-Merins seems hardly to leave room for the development of the humaner qualities; yet the flowering of Moroccan art and culture coincided with those tumultu-

ous years, and it was under the Merinid Sultans
that Fez became the centre of Moroccan learning
and industry, a kind of Oxford with Birmingham
annexed.

VI

THE SAADIANS

MEANWHILE, behind all the Berber turmoil a secret
work of religious propaganda was going on. The
Arab element had been crushed but not extirpated.
The crude idolatrous wealth-loving Berbers apparently dominated; but whenever there was a new
uprising or a new invasion it was based on the
religious discontent perpetually stirred up by Mahometan agents. The longing for a Mahdi, a Sa-
viour, the craving for purification combined with
an opportunity to murder and rob, always gave
the Moslem apostle a ready opening; and the down-
fall of the Merinids was the result of a long series
of religious movements to which the European invasion gave an object and a war-cry.

The Saadians were Cherifian Arabs, newcomers
from Arabia, to whom the lax Berber paganism
was abhorrent. They preached a return to the

creed of Mahomet, and proclaimed the Holy War against the hated Portuguese, who had set up fortified posts all along the west coast of Morocco.

It is a mistake to suppose that hatred of the Christian has always existed among the North African Moslems. The earlier dynasties, and especially the great Almohad Sultans, were on friendly terms with the Catholic powers of Europe, and in the thirteenth century a treaty assured to Christians in Africa full religious liberty, excepting only the right to preach their doctrine in public places. There was a Catholic diocese at Fez, and afterward at Marrakech under Gregory IX, and there is a letter of the Pope thanking the "Miromilan" (the Emir El Moumenin) for his kindness to the Bishop and the friars living in his dominions. Another Bishop was recommended by Innocent IV to the Sultan of Morocco; the Pope even asked that certain strongholds should be assigned to the Christians in Morocco as places of refuge in times of disturbance. But the best proof of the friendly relations between Christians and infidels is the fact that the Christian armies which helped the Sultans of Morocco to defeat Spain and subjugate Algeria and Tunisia were not composed of "renegadoes" or captives, as is generally supposed, but of Christian mercenaries, French and English, led by knights and nobles, and fighting for the Sultan of Morocco exactly as they would have fought for the Duke of Burgundy, the Count of Flanders, or any other Prince who offered high pay and held out the hope of rich spoils. Any one who has read "Villehardouin" and "Joinville" will own that there is not much to choose between the motives animating these noble freebooters and those which caused the Crusaders to loot Constantinople "on the way" to the Holy Sepulchre. War in those days was regarded as a lucrative and legitimate form of business, exactly as it was when the earlier heroes started out to take the rich robber-town of Troy.

The Berbers have never been religious fanatics, and the Vicomte de Foucauld, when he made his great journey of exploration in the Atlas in 1883, remarked that antagonism to the foreigner was always due to the fear of military espionage and never to religious motives. This equally applies to the Berbers of the sixteenth century, when the Holy War against Catholic Spain and Portugal was preached. The real cause of the sudden deadly hatred of the foreigner was twofold. The Spaniards were detested because of the ferocious cruelty with which they had driven the Moors from Spain under Ferdinand and Isabella; and the Portuguese because of the arrogance and brutality of their military colonists in the fortified trading stations of the west coast. And both were feared as possible conquerors and overlords.

There was a third incentive also: the Moroccans, dealing in black slaves for the European market, had discovered the value of white slaves in Moslem markets. The Sultan had his fleet, and each coast-town its powerful pirate vessels, and from pirate-nests like Salé and Tangier the raiders continued, till well on into the first half of the nineteenth century, to seize European ships and carry their passengers to the slave-markets of Fez and Marrakech.* The miseries endured by these captives, and so poignantly described in John Windus's travels, and in the "Naufrage du Brick Sophie" by Charles Cochelet,† show how savage the feeling against the foreigner had become.

* The Moroccans being very poor seamen, these corsair-vessels were usually commanded and manned by Christian renegadoes and Turks.

† Cochelet was wrecked on the coast near Agadir early in the nineteenth century and was taken with his fellow-travellers overland to El-Ksar and Tangier, enduring terrible hardships by the way.

With the advent of the Cherifian dynasties, which coincided with this religious reform, and was in fact brought about by it, Morocco became a closed country, as fiercely guarded as Japan against European penetration. Cut off from civilizing influences, the Moslems isolated themselves in a lonely fanaticism, far more racial than religious, and the history of the country from the fall of the Merinids till the French annexation is mainly a dull tale of tribal warfare.

The religious movement of the sixteenth century was led and fed by zealots from the Sahara. One of them took possession of Rabat and Azemmour, and preached the Holy War; other "feudal fiefs" (as M. Augustin Bernard has well called them) were founded at Tameslout, Ilegh, Tamgrout: the tombs of the *marabouts* who led these revolts are scattered all along the west coast, and are still objects of popular veneration. The unorthodox saint worship which marks Moroccan Moslemism, and is commemorated by the countless white *koubbas* throughout the country, grew up chiefly at the time of the religious revival under the Saadian dynasty, and almost all the "Moulays" and "Sidis" ven-

erated between Tangier and the Atlas were warrior monks who issued forth from their fortified
Zaouias to drive the Christians out of Africa.

The Saadians were probably rather embarrassed
by these fanatics, whom they found useful to op-
pose to the Merinids, but troublesome where their
own plans were concerned. They were ambitious
and luxury-loving princes, who invaded the wealthy
kingdom of the Soudan, conquered the Sultan of
Timbuctoo, and came back laden with slaves and
gold to embellish Marrakech and spend their treasure in the usual demoralizing orgies. Their exquisite tombs at Marrakech commemorate in
courtly language the superhuman virtues of a
series of rulers whose debaucheries and vices were
usually cut short by assassination. Finally another
austere and fanatical mountain tribe surged down
on them, wiped them out, and ruled in their stead.

VII

THE HASSANIANS

THE new rulers came from the Tafilelt, which has always been a troublesome corner of Morocco. The first two Hassanian Sultans were the usual tribal chiefs bent on taking advantage of Saadian misrule to loot and conquer. But the third was the great Moulay-Ismaël, the tale of whose long and triumphant rule (1672 to 1727) has already been told in the chapter on Meknez. This savage and enlightened old man once more drew order out of anarchy, and left, when he died, an organized and administered empire, as well as a progeny of seven hundred sons and unnumbered daughters.*

The empire fell apart as usual, and no less quickly than usual, under his successors; and from his death until the strong hand of General Lyautey took over the direction of affairs the Hassanian

---

* Moulay-Ismaël was a learned theologian and often held religious discussions with the Fathers of the Order of Mercy and the Trinitarians. He was scrupulously orthodox in his religious observances, and wrote a treatise in defense of his faith which he sent to James II of England, urging him to become a Mahometan He invented most of the most exquisite forms of torture which subsequent Sultans have applied to their victims (see Loti, *Au Maroc*), and was fond of flowers, and extremely simple and frugal in his personal habits.

rule in Morocco was little more than a tumult of incoherent ambitions. The successors of Moulay-Ismaël inherited his blood-lust and his passion for dominion without his capacity to govern. In 1757 Sidi-Mohammed, one of his sons, tried to put order into his kingdom, and drove the last Portuguese out of Morocco; but under his successors the country remained isolated and stagnant, making spasmodic efforts to defend itself against the encroachments of European influence, while its rulers wasted their energy in a policy of double-dealing and dissimulation. Early in the nineteenth century the government was compelled by the European powers to suppress piracy and the trade in Christian slaves; and in 1830 the French conquest of Algeria broke down the wall of isolation behind which the country was mouldering away by placing a European power on one of its frontiers.

At first the conquest of Algeria tended to create a link between France and Morocco. The Dey of Algiers was a Turk, and, therefore, an hereditary enemy; and Morocco was disposed to favour the power which had broken Turkish rule in a neighbouring country. But the Sultan could not help trying to profit by the general disturbance to seize Tlemcen and raise insurrections in western Algeria; and presently Morocco was engaged in a Holy War against France. Abd-el-Kader, the Sultan of Algeria, had taken refuge in Morocco, and the Sultan of Morocco having furnished him with supplies and munitions, France sent an official remonstrance. At the same time Marshal Bugeaud landed at Mers-el-Kebir, and invited the Makhzen to discuss the situation. The offer was accepted and General Bedeau and the Caïd El Guennaoui met in an open place. Behind them their respective troops were drawn up, and almost as soon as the first salutes were exchanged the Caïd declared the negotiations broken off. The French troops accordingly withdrew to the coast, but during their retreat they were attacked by the Moroccans. This put an end to peaceful negotiations, and Tangier was besieged and taken. The following August Bugeaud brought his troops up from Oudjda, through the defile that leads from West Algeria, and routed the Moroccans. He wished to advance on Fez, but international politics interfered, and he was not allowed to carry out his plans. England looked unfavour-

ably on the French penetration of Morocco, and it
became necessary to conclude peace at once to
prove that France had no territorial ambitions
west of Oudjda.

Meanwhile a great Sultan was once more to appear in the land. Moulay-el-Hassan, who ruled
from 1873 to 1894, was an able and energetic administrator. He pieced together his broken empire, asserted his authority in Fez and Marrakech,
and fought the rebellious tribes of the west. In
1877 he asked the French government to send
him a permanent military mission to assist in
organizing his army. He planned an expedition
to the Souss, but the want of food and water in
the wilderness traversed by the army caused the
most cruel sufferings. Moulay-el-Hassan had provisions sent by sea, but the weather was too stormy
to allow of a landing on the exposed Atlantic coast,
and the Sultan, who had never seen the sea, was
as surprised and indignant as Canute to find that
the waves would not obey him.

His son Abd-el-Aziz was only thirteen years old
when he succeeded to the throne. For six years
he remained under the guardianship of Ba-Ahmed,
the black Vizier of Moulay-el-Hassan, who built

the fairy palace of the Bahia at Marrakech, with its mysterious pale green padlocked door leading down to the secret vaults where his treasure was hidden. When the all-powerful Ba-Ahmed died the young Sultan was nineteen. He was intelligent, charming, and fond of the society of Europeans; but he was indifferent to religious questions and still more to military affairs, and thus doubly at the mercy of native mistrust and European intrigue.

Some clumsy attempts at fiscal reform, and a too great leaning toward European habits and associates, roused the animosity of the people, and of the conservative party in the upper class. The Sultan's eldest brother, who had been set aside in his favour, was intriguing against him; the usual Cherifian Pretender was stirring up the factious tribes in the mountains; and the European powers were attempting, in the confusion of an ungoverned country, to assert their respective ascendencies.

The demoralized condition of the country justified these attempts, and made European interference inevitable. But the powers were jealously watching each other, and Germany, already covet-

ing the certain agricultural resources and the con-
jectured mineral wealth of Morocco, was above all
determined that a French protectorate should not
be set up.

In 1908 another son of Moulay-Hassan, Abd-el-
Hafid, was proclaimed Sultan by the reactionary
Islamite faction, who accused Abd-el-Aziz of having sold his country to the Christians. Abd-el-Aziz
was defeated in a battle near Marrakech, and retired to Tangier, where he still lives in futile state.
Abd-el-Hafid, proclaimed Sultan at Fez, was rec-
ognized by the whole country; but he found himself unable to cope with the factious tribes (those
outside the Blad-el-Makhzen, or *governed country*).
These rebel tribes besieged Fez, and the Sultan
had to ask France for aid. France sent troops to
his relief, but as soon as the dissidents were routed,
and he himself was safe, Abd-el-Hafid refused to
give the French army his support, and in 1912,
after the horrible massacres of Fez, he abdicated
in favour of another brother, Moulay Youssef, the
actual ruler of Morocco.

VIII

NOTE ON MOROCCAN ARCHITECTURE

NOTE ON MOROCCAN
ARCHITECTURE

I

M. SALADIN, whose "Manual of Moslem Architecture" was published in 1907, ends his chapter on Morocco with the words: "It is especially urgent that we should know, and penetrate into, Morocco as soon as possible, in order to study its monuments. It is the only country but Persia where Moslem art actually survives; and the tradition handed down to the present day will doubtless clear up many things."

M. Saladin's wish has been partly realized. Much has been done since 1912, when General Lyautey was appointed Resident-General, to clear up and classify the history of Moroccan art; but since 1914, though the work has never been dropped, it has necessarily been much delayed, especially as regards its published record; and as yet only a few monographs and articles have summed up some of the interesting investigations of the last five years.

II

WHEN I was in Marrakech word was sent to Captain de S., who was with me, that a Caïd of the Atlas, whose prisoner he had been several years before, had himself been taken by the Pasha's troops, and was in Marrakech. Captain de S. was asked to identify several rifles which his old enemy had taken from him, and on receiving them found that, in the interval, they had been elaborately ornamented with the Arab niello work of which the tradition goes back to Damascus.

This little incident is a good example of the degree to which the mediæval tradition alluded to by M. Saladin has survived in Moroccan life. Nowhere else in the world, except among the moribund fresco-painters of the Greek monasteries, has a formula of art persisted from the seventh or eighth century to the present day; and in Morocco the formula is not the mechanical expression of a petrified theology but the setting of the life of a

Marrakech—a street fountain

people who have gone on wearing the same clothes, observing the same customs, believing in the same fetiches, and using the same saddles, ploughs, looms, and dye-stuffs as in the days when the foundations of the first mosque of El Kairouiyin were laid.

The origin of this tradition is confused and obscure. The Arabs have never been creative artists, nor are the Berbers known to have been so. As investigations proceed in Syria and Mesopotamia it seems more and more probable that the sources of inspiration of pre-Moslem art in North Africa are to be found in Egypt, Persia, and India. Each new investigation pushes these sources farther back and farther east; but it is not of much use to retrace these ancient vestiges, since Moroccan art has, so far, nothing to show of pre-Islamite art, save what is purely Phenician or Roman.

In any case, however, it is not in Morocco that the clue to Moroccan art is to be sought; though interesting hints and mysterious reminiscences will doubtless be found in such places as Tinmel, in the gorges of the Atlas, where a ruined mosque of the earliest Almohad period has been photographed by

M. Doutté, and in the curious Algerian towns of Sedrata and the Kalaa of the Beni Hammads. Both of these latter towns were rich and prosperous communities in the tenth century and both were destroyed in the eleventh, so that they survive as mediæval Pompeiis of a quite exceptional interest, since their architecture appears to have been almost unaffected by classic or Byzantine influences.

Traces of a very old indigenous art are found in the designs on the modern white and black Berber pottery; but this work, specimens of which are to be seen in the Oriental Department of the Louvre, seems to go back, by way of Central America, Greece (sixth century B. C.) and Susa (twelfth century B. C.), to the far-off period before the streams of human invention had divided, and when the same loops and ripples and spirals formed on the flowing surface of every current.

It is a disputed question whether Spanish influence was foremost in developing the peculiarly Moroccan art of the earliest Moslem period, or whether European influences came by way of Syria and Palestine, and afterward met and were crossed with those of Moorish Spain. Probably both things happened, since the Almoravids were in Spain; and no doubt the currents met and mingled. At any rate, Byzantine, Greece, and the Palestine and Syria of the Crusaders, contributed as much as Rome and Greece to the formation of that peculiar Moslem art which, all the way from India to the Pillars of Hercules, built itself, with minor variations, out of the same elements.

Arab conquerors always destroy as much as they can of the work of their predecessors, and nothing remains, as far as is known, of Almoravid architecture in Morocco. But the great Almohad Sultans covered Spain and Northwest Africa with their monuments, and no later buildings in Africa equal them in strength and majesty.

It is no doubt because the Almohads built in stone that so much of what they made survives. The Merinids took to rubble and a soft tufa, and the Cherifian dynasties built in clay like the Spaniards in South America. And so seventeenth century Meknez has perished while the Almohad walls and towers of the tenth century still stand.

The principal old buildings of Morocco are defensive and religious—and under the latter term the beautiful collegiate houses (the medersas) of Fez and Salé may fairly be included, since the educational system of Islam is essentially and fundamentally theological. Of old secular buildings, palaces or private houses, virtually none are known to exist; but their plan and decorations may easily be reconstituted from the early chronicles, and also from the surviving palaces built in the eighteenth and nineteenth centuries, and even those which the wealthy nobles of modern Morocco are building to this day.

The whole of civilian Moslem architecture from Persia to Morocco is based on four unchanging conditions: a hot climate, slavery, polygamy and the segregation of women. The private house in Mahometan countries is in fact a fortress, a convent and a temple: a temple of which the god (as in all ancient religions) frequently descends to visit his cloistered votaresses. For where slavery and polygamy exist every house-master is necessarily a god, and the house he inhabits a shrine built about his divinity.

The first thought of the Moroccan chieftain was always defensive. As soon as he pitched a camp

From a photograph from the Service des Beaux-Arts au Maroc

Rabat—gate of the Kasbah of the Oudayas

or founded a city it had to be guarded against the hungry hordes who encompassed him on every side. Each little centre of culture and luxury in Moghreb was an islet in a sea of perpetual storms. The wonder is that, thus incessantly threatened from without and conspired against from within—with the desert at their doors, and their slaves on the threshold—these violent men managed to create about them an atmosphere of luxury and stability that astonished not only the obsequious native chronicler but travellers and captives from western Europe.

The truth is, as has been often pointed out, that, even until the end of the seventeenth century, the refinements of civilization were in many respects no greater in France and England than in North Africa. North Africa had long been in more direct communication with the old Empires of immemorial luxury, and was therefore farther advanced in the arts of living than the Spain and France of the Dark Ages; and this is why, in a country that to the average modern European seems as savage as Ashantee, one finds traces of a refinement of life and taste hardly to be matched by Carlovingian and early Capetian Europe.

III

THE brief Almoravid dynasty left no monuments behind it.

Fez had already been founded by the Idrissites, and its first mosques (Kairouiyin and Les Andalous) existed. Of the Almoravid Fez and Marrakech the chroniclers relate great things; but the wild Hilalian invasion and the subsequent descent of the Almohads from the High Atlas swept away whatever the first dynasties had created.

The Almohads were mighty builders, and their great monuments are all of stone. The earliest known example of their architecture which has survived is the ruined mosque of Tinmel, in the High Atlas, discovered and photographed by M. Doutté. This mosque was built by the inspired mystic, Ibn-Toumert, who founded the line. Following him came the great palace-making Sultans whose walled cities of splendid mosques and towers have Romanesque qualities of mass and proportion, and, as M. Raymond Koechlin has pointed out, inevitably recall the "robust simplicity of the master builders who at the very same moment

From a photograph from the Service des Beaux-Arts au Maroc

Fez —Medersa Bouanyana

were beginning in France the construction of the first Gothic cathedrals and the noblest feudal castles."

In the thirteenth century, with the coming of the Merinids, Moroccan architecture grew more delicate, more luxurious, and perhaps also more peculiarly itself. That interaction of Spanish and Arab art which produced the style known as Moorish reached, on the African side of the Straits, its greatest completeness in Morocco. It was under the Merinids that Moorish art grew into full beauty in Spain, and under the Merinids that Fez rebuilt the mosque Kairouiyin and that of the Andalusians, and created six of its nine *Medersas*, the most perfect surviving buildings of that unique moment of sober elegance and dignity.

The Cherifian dynasties brought with them a decline in taste. A crude desire for immediate effect, and the tendency toward a more barbaric luxury, resulted in the piling up of frail palaces as impermanent as tents. Yet a last flower grew from the deformed and dying trunk of the old Empire. The Saadian Sultan who invaded the Soudan and came back laden with gold and treasure from

the great black city of Timbuctoo covered Marrakech with hasty monuments of which hardly a
trace survives. But there, in a nettle-grown corner
of a ruinous quarter, lay hidden till yesterday the
Chapel of the Tombs: the last emanation of pure
beauty of a mysterious, incomplete, forever retro-
gressive and yet forever forward-straining people.
The Merinid tombs of Fez have fallen; but those
of their destroyers linger on in precarious grace,
like a flower on the edge of a precipice.

IV

MOROCCAN architecture, then, is easily divided into
four groups: the fortress, the mosque, the collegiate
building and the private house.

The kernel of the mosque is always the *mihrab*,
or niche facing toward the Kasbah of Mecca, where
the *imam** stands to say the prayer. This arrange-
ment, which enabled as many as possible of the
faithful to kneel facing the *mihrab*, results in a
ground-plan necessarily consisting of long aisles
parallel with the wall of the *mihrab*, to which more

* The "deacon" or elder of the Moslem religion, which has no order of
priests.

From a photograph from the Service des Beaux-Arts au Maroc

Fez—the praying-chapel in the Medersa el Attarine

and more aisles are added as the number of worshippers grows. Where there was not space to
increase these lateral aisles they were lengthened
at each end. This typical plan is modified in the
Moroccan mosques by a wider transverse space,
corresponding with the nave of a Christian church,
and extending across the mosque from the praying
niche to the principal door. To the right of the
mihrab is the *minbar*, the carved pulpit (usually of
cedar-wood incrusted with mother-of-pearl and
ebony) from which the Koran is read. In some
Algerian and Egyptian mosques (and at Cordova,
for instance) the *mihrab* is enclosed in a sort of
screen called the *maksoura;* but in Morocco this
modification of the simpler plan was apparently
not adopted.

The interior construction of the mosque was no
doubt usually affected by the nearness of Roman
or Byzantine ruins. M. Saladin points out that
there seem to be few instances of the use of columns
made by native builders; but it does not therefore
follow that all the columns used in the early mosques
were taken from Roman temples or Christian basil-
icas. The Arab invaders brought their architects

and engineers with them; and it is very possible that some of the earlier mosques were built by prisoners or fortune-hunters from Greece or Italy or Spain.

At any rate, the column on which the arcades of the vaulting rests in the earlier mosques, as at Tunis and Kairouan, and the mosque El Kairoui-yin at Fez, gives way later to the use of piers, foursquare, or with flanking engaged pilasters as at Algiers and Tlemcen. The exterior of the mosques, as a rule, is almost entirely hidden by a mushroom growth of buildings, lanes and covered bazaars; but where the outer walls have remained disengaged they show, as at Kairouan and Cordova, great masses of windowless masonry pierced at intervals with majestic gateways.

Beyond the mosque, and opening into it by many wide doors of beaten bronze or carved cedarwood, lies the Court of the Ablutions. The openings in the façade were multiplied in order that, on great days, the faithful who were not able to enter the mosque might hear the prayers and catch a glimpse of the *mihrab*.

In a corner of the courts stands the minaret. It

is the structure on which Moslem art has played
the greatest number of variations, cutting off its
angles, building it on a circular or polygonal plan,
and endlessly modifying the pyramids and pendentives by which the ground-plan of one story passes
into that of the next. These problems of transition, always fascinating to the architect, led in Persia, Mesopotamia and Egypt to many different
compositions and ways of treatment; but in Morocco the minaret, till modern times, remained
steadfastly square, and proved that no other plan
is so beautiful as this simplest one of all.

Surrounding the Court of the Ablutions are the
school-rooms, libraries and other dependencies,
which grew as the Mahometan religion prospered
and Arab culture developed.

The medersa was a farther extension of the
mosque: it was the academy where the Moslem
schoolman prepared his theology and the other
branches of strange learning which, to the present
day, make up the curriculum of the Mahometan
university. The medersa is an adaptation of the
private house to religious and educational ends; or,
if one prefers another analogy, it is a *fondak* built

above a miniature mosque. The ground-plan is always the same: in the centre an arcaded court with a fountain, on one side the long narrow praying-chapel with the *mihrab*, on the other a class-room with the same ground-plan; and on the next story a series of cell-like rooms for the students,. opening on carved cedar-wood balconies. This cloistered plan, where all the effect is reserved for the interior façades about the court, lends itself to a delicacy of detail that would be inappropriate on a street-front; and the medersas of Fez are endlessly varied in their fanciful but never exuberant decoration.

M. Tranchant de Lunel has pointed out (in "France-Maroc") with what a sure sense of suitability the Merinid architects adapted this decoration to the uses of the buildings. On the lower floor, under the cloister, is a revêtement of marble (often alabaster) or of the almost indestructible ceramic mosaic.* On the floor above, massive cedar-wood corbels ending in monsters of almost Gothic inspiration support the fretted balconies;

* These Moroccan mosaics are called *zellyes*.

Salé—interior court of the Medersa

and above rise stucco interlacings, placed too high up to be injured by man, and guarded from the weather by projecting eaves.

The private house, whether merchant's dwelling or chieftain's palace, is laid out on the same lines, with the addition of the reserved quarters for women; and what remains in Spain and Sicily of Moorish secular architecture shows that, in the Merinid period, the play of ornament must have been—as was natural—even greater than in the medersas.

The Arab chroniclers paint pictures of Merinid palaces, such as the House of the Favourite at Cordova, which the soberer modern imagination refused to accept until the medersas of Fez were revealed, and the old decorative tradition was shown in the eighteenth century Moroccan palaces. The descriptions given of the palaces of Fez and of Marrakech in the preceding articles, which make it unnecessary, in so slight a note as this, to go again into the detail of their planning and decoration, will serve to show how gracefully the art of the mosque and the medersa was lightened and domesticated to suit these cool chambers and flower-filled courts.

With regard to the immense fortifications that are the most picturesque and noticeable architectural features of Morocco, the first thing to strike the traveller is the difficulty of discerning any difference in the probable date of their construction until certain structural peculiarities are examined, or the ornamental details of the great gateways are noted. Thus the Almohad portions of the walls of Fez and Rabat are built of stone, while later parts are of rubble; and the touch of European influence in certain gateways of Meknez and Fez at once situate them in the seventeenth century. But the mediæval outline of these great piles of masonry, and certain technicalities in their plan, such as the disposition of the towers, alternating in the inner and outer walls, continued unchanged throughout the different dynasties; and this immutability of the Moroccan military architecture enables the imagination to picture, not only what was the aspect of the fortified cities which the Greeks built in Palestine and Syria, and the Crusaders brought back

[276]

From a Photograph from the Service des Beaux-Arts au Maroc

Marrakech—the gate of the Portuguese

to Europe, but even that of the far-off Assyrio-Chaldæan strongholds to which the whole fortified architecture of the Middle Ages in Europe seems to lead back.

IX
BOOKS CONSULTED

IX

BOOKS CONSULTED

Afrique Française (L'), Bulletin Mensuel du Comité de l'Afrique Française. Paris, 21, rue Cassette.

Bernard, Augustin. Le Maroc. Paris, F. Alcan, 1916.

Budgett-Meakin. The Land of the Moors. London, 1902.

Châtelain, L. Recherches archéologiques au Maroc. Volubilis. (Published by the Military Command in Morocco)

Les Fouilles de Volubilis. (Extrait du Bulletin Archéologique, 1916.)

Chevrillon, A. Crépuscule d'Islam.

Cochelet, Charles Le Naufrage du Brick Sophie.

Conférences Marocaines. Paris, Plon-Nourrit.

Doutté, E. En Tribu. Paris, 1914.

Foucauld, Vicomte de. La Reconnaissance au Maroc. Paris, 1888.

France-Maroc. Revue Mensuelle, Paris, 4, rue Chauveau-Lagarde.

Gaillard Une Ville d'Islam, Fez. Paris, 1909.

Gayet, Al. L'Art Arabe Paris, 1906.

Houdas, O. Le Maroc de 1631 à 1812. Extrait d'une histoire du Maroc intitulée "L'Interprète qui s'exprime clairement sur les dynasties de l'Orient et de l'Occident" par Ezziani. Paris, E. Leroux, 1886.

BOOKS CONSULTED

Koechlin, Raymond. Une Exposition d'Art Marocain. (Gazette des Beaux-Arts, Juillet-Septembre, 1917.)

Leo Africanus, Description of Africa.

Loti, Pierre. Au Maroc.

Migeon, Gaston. Manuel d'Art Musulman. II. Les Arts Plastiques et Industriels. Paris, A. Picard et Fils, 1907.

Saladin, H. Manuel d'Art Musulman. I. L'Architecture. Paris, A. Picard et Fils, 1907.

Segonzac, Marquis de. Voyages au Maroc. Paris, 1903. Au Cœur de l'Atlas. Paris, 1910.

Tarde, A. de. Les Villes du Maroc: Fez, Marrakech, Rabat. (Journal de l'Université des Annales, 15 Oct., 1 Nov., 1918.)

Windus. A Journey to Mequinez. London, 1721.

INDEX

INDEX

INDEX

INDEX

INDEX

appointed Resident-General in Morocco, 210

military occupation of Morocco by, 211, 212

policy of, 213 *et seq.*

economic development of Morocco achieved by, 218-222

summary of work of, 222-226

Maclean, Sir Harry, 144

Mamora, forest of, 14

Mangin, General, 212

Mansourah, mosque of, 150

Market, of Marrakech, 144

in Moulay Idriss, 49

of Salé, 26, 27

of Sefrou, 111-113

Marrakech, the road to, 123-126

founders of, 128, 129, 242

tower of the Koutoubya at, 127, 128

palace of the Bahia at, 129-133

the lamp-lighters of, 133

mixed population of, 134

bazaars of, 135-138

the "morocco" workers of, 137

olive-yards of, 139

the Menara of, 139, 140

a holiday of merchants of, 140-142

the Square of the Dead in, 143-145

French administration office at, 144

fruit-market of, 144

dance of Chleuh boys in, 148

Saadian tombs of, 149, 154-158, 252

a harem in, 197-205

taken by the French, 212

Catholic diocese at, 248

Chapel of the Tombs at, 270

Medersa, the, of the Oudayas, 19-22

Attarine, 99

at Fez, 99, 105-107

at Salé, 25, 26

architecture of, 273-275

Mehedyia, Phenician colony of, 38, 237

Meknez, building of, 57-64, 69, 70

the Kasbah of, 62

palaces of, 63

stables of, 63

entrance into, 64

ruins of, 64-66

sunken gardens of, 72

visit of English emissaries to, 71-73

Mellah, of Fez, 113

of Sefrou, 113-116

Menara, the, in the Agdal, 139, 140

Mequinez. *See* Meknez

Merinids, the, tombs of, at Fez, 78, 79

conquest of Morocco by, 245-247

architecture of, 269, 274, 275

Mirador, the Imperial, 170-181

Moorish art, 269

Mosque, of Elakhador, 62

of El Andalous, 101, 102, 240, 268, 269

of El Kairouiyin, 80, 83, 93-100, 240, 263, 268, 269

of Kairouan, 93

of Mansourah, 150

of Rabat, 32

of Tinmel, 243, 268

of Tunisia, 96

architecture of Moroccan, 270-273

Moulay Hafid, 81

Moulay-el-Hassan, 129, 256

Moulay Idriss I, rule of, 239

tomb of, 94

Moulay Idriss II, tomb of, 61, 80, 83, 94

rule of, 240

Moulay Idriss, Sacred City of, 5, 39, 45-57

Street of the Weavers in, 47

INDEX

INDEX

CPSIA information can be obtained
at www.ICGtesting.com
Printed in the USA
BVHW041000020719
552485BV00013B/497/P